2015

China Mineral Resources

Ministry of Land and Resources
People's Republic of China

GEOLOGICAL PUBLISHING HOUSE
BEIJING
October, 2015

Editorial Committee

Foreword

In 2014, China has continued the implementation of *National Exploration and Development Planning* and achieved outstanding progress in geological prospecting, and it is the reserves & resources of major mineral resources that increased obviously. There is a sustainable growth in the production and import of major mineral products as well as a further improvement in the supplying capacity. Efforts have been made to promote the survey and evaluation of geology and mineral resources, and better social services. To facilitate the construction of ecological civilization, China has paid more attention to enhance the environmental recovery of mines, and over 25% of the land damaged by mining development has been reclaimed.

Chinese government has further streamlined the administration, taken multiple measures to stimulate the market, standardized the management of mineral resources, and achieved progress in the conservation and comprehensive utilization. Since 2014, China has canceled 23 examinations and approvals pertaining to geology and mineral resources, brought the mineral resources compensation rate of coal, oil and natural gas to zero and applied ad valorem collection of resource tax on coal. In addition, China has released the first index criterion for the comprehensive utilization of mineral resources and the minimum index requirements for the extract recovery rate, concentration recovery rate and comprehensive utilization rate of 8 minerals.

Ministry of Land and Resources has formulated the Report on China Mineral Resources since 2011, in order to make the public better understanding the situation of exploration and exploitation of mineral resources, obtain more knowledge on the policies regarding the management of mineral resources, and enhance the capacity of public service and impel the opening of administrative information. This report systematically analyzes the situation of mineral resources, emphatically introduces the main progress in surveys and evaluations of geology and mineral resources, exploration, development and utilization of mineral resources, mine ecological civilization construction and management of mineral resources in China since 2014; reflects the dynamic state of mineral resources management from the perspectives of mineral resources planning, exploration & mining rights, reserves, exploration, supervision and so on; expounds the reform progress and essential policies from the perspectives of the construction of policy system, reform of taxes and charges; presents the latest progress of China's technical innovation of geology and mining from the perspectives of geological theories and technologies of exploration and exploitation; summarizes the situation of international cooperation on mineral resources.

We hope this report will be an important way to know of and understand the general situation of mineral resources in China for those who care for and support the country's undertaking of mineral resources.

The statistical data of this report are mainly sourced from the National Bureau of Statistics, the Ministry of Land and Resources and the General Administration of Customs of the People's Republic of China, excluding those of the Hong Kong Special Administrative Region, the Macau Special Administrative Region and Taiwan Province.

Contents

Chapter I Situation of Mineral Resources 1

Chapter II Status of Mineral Resources 4

I. Reserves & Resources 4

II. Potential of Mineral Resources 7

III. Registration of Exploration and Mining Rights 9

Chapter III Exploration 10

I. Exploration Investment 10

II. Energy Mineral Exploration 11

III. Exploration of Metallic and Non-metallic Minerals 12

IV. Groundwater Exploration 13

Chapter IV Development and Utilization of Mineral Resources 14

I. Mining Fixed Assets Investment 14

II. Production and Consumption 15

III. Conservation and Comprehensive Utilization 17

Chapter V Mine Ecological Environment Construction 22

I. Geological Environment Restoration 22

II. Green Mining Development 23

Chapter VI Mineral Resources Management and Policies 24

I. Items Subject to Administrative Examination and Approval 24

II. Taxes and Fees 30

III. Mineral Resources Planning 32
IV. Management of Exploration and Mining Rights 32
V. Management of Geological Survey Qualifications 33

Chapter VII Geological Survey and Geological Data Service 36

I. Basic Geological Survey 36
II. Survey and Evaluation of Mineral Resources 37
III. Geological Data Management and Service 39

Chapter VIII Scientific and Technological Innovation and International Cooperation................................ 42

I. Basic Geological and Mineral Theoretical Research.............................. 42
II. Techniques of Mineral Exploration, Exploitation and Utilization 43
III. Technical Standards for Geology and Mineral Resources 44
IV. International Cooperation 45

Chapter I
Situation of Mineral Resources

The global mining industry has witnessed a continuing depression along with the economic rebalancing and a weak demand for mineral products, which has been challenging the globe since 2014. At the same time, China has entered the phase of adjustment in its mining development. In order to stimulate market and propel the transformation and upgrading of the mining industry, Chinese government has intensified the geological exploration and improved the conservation and comprehensive utilization of mineral resources, streamlined the administration and improved social service.

Deep comprehension of mineral resources potential. In 2014, China has spent RMB114.5 billion on geological exploration, and there are 249 newly-discovered large and medium-sized ore fields. Significant breakthroughs have been made in the exploration of oil and gas resources, and the geological reserves of shale gas 106.8 billion cubic meters first reported. The newly-discovered geological reserves of oil are 1.06 billion tons and those of natural gas reach 943.8 billion cubic meters. In the 45 major minerals, the reserves & resources of 36 minerals increase, among which the remaining technically recoverable reserves of oil rise by 2.0% and those of natural gas increased by 6.5%; the reserves & resources of coal grow by 3.2% and those of iron ore increased by 5.6%, copper 6.3%, bauxite 3.2% and gold 9.4%. The latest dynamic evaluation on oil and gas resources indicates that geological resources of oil have reached 108.5 billion tons, natural gas 68 trillion cubic meters, shale gas 134 trillion cubic meters, and coal-bed methane 36.8 trillion cubic meters. The potential evaluation of 25 major minerals shows the average discovery rate of mineral resources is 30.3%, indicating a huge prospecting potential. The potential of coal resources at depth shallow than 2,000m is 3.88 trillion tons, with a discovery rate of 29.6%. That of iron ore is 196.0 billion tons, with a discovery rate of 33.1%; copper 304 million tons, with a discovery rate of 29.5%; and bauxite 17.97 billion tons, with a discovery rate of 20.3%.

Conservation and comprehensive utilization of mineral resources enhanced. In 2014, the output of primary energies, crude steel, ten non-ferrous metals and gold ranks top in the world. The output of primary energies is 3.60 billion tons of standard coal equivalents, among which the output of raw coal is 3.87 billion tons, crude oil 211 million tons and natural gas 130.16 billion cubic meters, and the consumption of primary energies is 4.26 billion tons of standard coal equivalents, with a self-sufficiency rate of 84.5%. The output of crude steel amounts to 820 million tons, that of ten non-ferrous metals is 43.801 million tons and that of gold is 458.1 tons. In the same year, the country's total volume of mineral products trade is US$1.09 trillion, with an increasing of 5.7% year-on-year, among which 291 million tons of coal have been imported, with a drop of 10.9%; oil 338 million tons, with a growth of 5.1%; and iron ore 933 million tons, with an increase of 13.8%. The standard for the indexes of evaluating the comprehensive utilization of mineral resources has been formulated and released. China has enacted the index requirements for the extract recovery rate, concentration recovery rate and comprehensive utilization rate of 20 minerals in three consecutive years and the evaluation index system for the conservation and comprehensive utilization of major mineral resources has been initially established. Besides, 159 recommended technologies have been popularized in three consecutive years. Furthermore, efforts have been made to propel the construction of pilot bases for the comprehensive utilization and the mine geological environment restoration projects of resource-exhausted cities and relevant demonstration projects. 661 mining enterprises have been selected in four batches to serve as the nation-level pilot entities for green mines.

The administrative policies of mineral resources further improved. Chinese government has revised the administrative regulations regarding the registration of exploration and exploitation, the transfer of exploration and mining rights and so on, released the Administrative Regulations on Geological Environment Monitoring and the Administrative Penalty Measures on Land and Resources, cancelled 23 examinations and approvals pertaining to mineral resources, put mineral resource compensation rates for coal, crude oil and natural gas to zero and applied ad valorem collection of resource tax on coal.

Geological service further strengthened. By the end of 2014, onshore regional geological survey of 1:50,000 and regional geological revision of 1:250,000 has covered 31.7% and 61.7% the territorial area, respectively . The regional geological survey of 1:1,000,000 has covered the entire marine area under the jurisdiction of China for the first time. In 2014, over 170 wells has been both explored and exploited, benefiting 300,000 people in water-deficient area. The access for the geological data sharing and service platform reached 620,000 times and the national-level and the provincial-level geological data entities provided data services for 130,000 times. The Cores and Samples Center of Land and Resources provided services for 5,646 person-times.

As the economic development has entered into a "New Normal" stage and the GDP grows at a high- medium speed, China keeps a high demand for bulk minerals and a rapidly increasing demand for mineral resources relating to high-tech industries. Hence, the development of geological sectors should be transformed and upgraded and the management of mineral resources should adapt itself to the changing tendency. Additionally, constant efforts should be made to deepen the reform in the administrative system of mineral resources, attach significant importance to the support from science and technology and improve effectively the level of geological service.

Chapter II
Status of Mineral Resources

In 2014, evident growths have been witnessed in the newly-discovered reserves & resources of major minerals such as coal, oil, natural gas, shale gas, manganese ore, bauxite, gold, tungsten, molybdenum and so on. The geological reserves of shale gas were reported for the first time. The evaluation on the potential of 25 minerals has been completed, indicating a huge prospecting potential.

I. Reserves & Resources

1. Changes of reserves & resources

In 2014, among the 45 major minerals, the reserves & resources of 36 minerals increased, that of 5 decreased, and that of 4 remained unchanged. The geological reserves of shale gas were reported for the first time. A growth is witnessed in the reserves & resources of energy minerals and ferrous minerals. The remaining technically recoverable reserves of oil increased 2.0% year-on-year, and that of natural gas increased by 6.5%. The reserves & resources of coal increased by 3.2%, iron ore 5.6% and manganese ore 18.5%. Among non-ferrous minerals, the reserves & resources of copper increased by 6.3%, nickel 12.9% and lead 9.6%. Among precious metal minerals, the reserves & resources of gold increased by 9.4% and silver 6.3%. The reserves & resources of most nonmetallic minerals increased at different rates, with gypsum 18.4% and Potash 11.3%, while that of barite and diatomite declined (Table 2-1).

Table 2–1 Reserves & Resources of 45 Major Minerals

Name of Mineral	Unit	2013	2014	Increase or Decrease (%)
Coal	trillion tons	1.48	1.53	3.2
Oil	billion tons	3.37	3.43	2.0
Natural gas	trillion cubic meters	4.64	4.95	6.5
Shale gas	billion cubic meters	–	25.46	–
Iron ore	billion tons of ores	79.85	84.34	5.6
Manganese ore	billion tons of ores	1.03	1.22	18.5

Continued

Name of Mineral	Unit	2013	2014	Increase or Decrease (%)
Chromite	million tons of ores	11.42	11.62	1.8
Vanadium	V_2O_5 million tons	57.13	60.75	6.3
Titanium	TiO_2 million tons	760	762	0.9
Copper	million tons of metals	91.12	96.90	6.3
Lead	million tons of metals	67.37	73.85	9.6
Zinc	million tons of metals	137.38	144.86	5.5
Bauxite	billion tons of ores	4.02	4.15	3.2
Nickel	million tons of metals	9.01	10.17	12.9
Cobalt	thousand tons of metals	637.0	670.0	5.3
Tungsten	WO_3 million tons	7.014	7.205	2.7
Tin	million tons of metals	4.255	4.189	-1.6
Molybdenum	million tons of metals	26.20	28.26	7.9
Antimony	million tons of metals	2.629	2.840	8.0
Gold	Tons of metals	8974.7	9816.0	9.4
Silver	thousand tons of metals	223.0	237.0	6.3
Platinum group metal	tons of metals	372.4	372.3	-0.04
Strontium	million tons of celestine	45.67	45.67	0.0
Magnesite	billion tons of ores	2.89	2.91	0.7
Fluorite	million tons of minerals	211	223	5.7
Refractory clay	billion tons of ores	2.51	2.52	0.5
Pyrites	billion tons of ores	5.69	5.83	2.4
Phosphate rock	billion tons of ores	20.57	21.45	4.3
Potash	KCl billion tons	1.01	1.12	11.3
Boron	B_2O_3 million tons	76.136	76.225	0.1
Mirabilite	Na_2SO_4 billion tons	111.30	117.09	5.2
Barite	million tons of ores	312	305	-2.2
Cement-producing limestone	billion tons of ores	119.88	123.51	3.0
Glass-making siliceous-rock	billion tons of ores	7.34	7.58	3.3
Gypsum	billion tons of ores	85.04	100.72	18.4
Kaolin	billion tons of ores	2.50	2.67	6.5
Bentonite	billion tons of ores	2.80	2.87	2.7

Continued

Name of Mineral	Unit	2013	2014	Increase or Decrease (%)
Diatomite	billion tons of ores	0.47	0.45	-3.9
Veneer granite	billion cubic meters	2.59	2.67	3.2
Veneer marble	billion cubic meters	1.51	1.56	3.4
Diamond	kilograms of minerals	3396.5	3396.5	0.0
Crystalloid graphite	billion tons of minerals	0.22	0.22	0.0
Asbestos	million tons of minerals	90.724	91.646	1.0
Talc	million tons of ores	277	276	-0.4
Wollastonite	million tons of ores	160	160	0.0

Note: That of oil, natural gas and shale gas are the remaining technologically recoverable reserves.

"-" means there is no statistical data.

2. Newly discovered reserves & resources from exploration

In 2014, there are newly-discovered reserves & resources for important minerals in China. The newly-discovered technologically recoverable reserves of oil are 190 million tons, that of natural gas are 474.96 billion cubic meters and shale gas 26.69 billion cubic meters. The newly-discovered reserves & resources of coal are 56.1 billion tons, iron ore 4.3 billion tons, copper 4.95 million tons, lead 5.97 million tons, zinc 6.08 million tons, bauxite 180 million tons, tungsten 345 thousand tons, gold 836 tons, silver 15,000 tons, pyrite 176.46 million tons and phosphate rock 1.03 billion tons (Table 2-2).

Table 2-2 Newly-Discovered Reserves & Resources from Exploration

Minerals	Unit	2013	2014
Coal	billion tons	67.3	56.1
Oil	million tons	200	190
Natural gas	billion cubic meters	381.60	474.96
Shale gas	billion cubic meters	–	26.69
Iron ore	billion tons of ores	2.65	4.3
Manganese ore	million tons of ores	110	190
Copper	million tons of metals	2.61	4.95
Lead	million tons of metals	4.46	5.97
Zinc	million tons of metals	13.89	6.08

Continued

Minerals	Unit	2013	2014
Bauxite	million tons of ores	240	180
Gold	tons of gold	758	836
Silver	thousand tons of silver	13	15
Tungsten	WO_3 thousand tons	203	345
Tin	thousand tons of metals	130	8.7
Molybdenum	million tons of metals	4.61	1.98
Antimony	thousand tons of metals	137	246
Pyrite	million tons of ores	79.81	176.46
Phosphate rock	million tons of ores	440	1030
Potash	KCl million of tons	0	70.42

Note: That of petroleum, natural gas and shale gas is technologically recoverable reserves.

"-" means there is no statistical data.

II. Potential of Mineral Resources

1. Oil and gas

China's oil and gas resources distribute mainly on large petroliferous basins and 80% of its oil and gas resources, reserves and output are contributed by such major basins as Bohai Bay, Songliao, Tarim, Ordos, Junggar and Pearl River Estuary. The nationwide evaluation on conventional oil and gas resources potential indicates that by the end of 2014, the geological resources of oil were 108.5 billion tons, of which 26.8 billion tons were recoverable; conventional natural gas 68 trillion cubic meters, with 40 trillion cubic meters recoverable; shale gas 134 trillion cubic meters, with 25 trillion cubic meters recoverable; and coal-bed methane 36.8 trillion cubic meters, with 10.9 trillion cubic meters recoverable. In general, natural gas has a greater potential than oil. China's reserves and output of natural gas will witness a rapid growth in the future.

2. Solid minerals

The evaluation on the potential of the mineral resources, including coal, uranium, iron ore, manganese ore, chromite, copper, lead, zinc, bauxite, nickel, tungsten, tin, molybdenum, antimony, gold, silver, lithium, rare earth, magnesite, fluorite, sulfur, phosphate rock, potash, barite and boron, was completed in 2014. The evaluation shows that the discovery rate of major mineral resources is 30.3% in average, indicating a huge prospecting potential. The potential of coal resources at depth shallow than 2,000m is 3.88 trillion tons, with a discovery rate of 29.6%. That of iron ore is 196.0 billion tons, with a discovery rate of 33.1%; copper 304 million tons, with a discovery rate of 29.5%; and bauxite 17.97 billion tons, with a discovery rate of 20.3%(Table 2-3).

Table 2–3 Major Mineral Resources Potential

No.	Minerals	Unit	Predicted Resources	Discovery Rate/ %
1	Coal	trillion tons	3.88	29.6
2	Iron ore	billion tons of ores	196	33.1
3	Manganese ore	billion tons of ores	3.52	31.7
4	Chromite	million tons of ores	55.56	23.6
5	Copper	million tons of metals	304	29.5
6	Lead	million tons of metals	235	30.5
7	Zinc	million tons of metals	511	28.9
8	Bauxite	billion tons of ores	17.97	20.3
9	Nickel	million tons of metals	24.51	34.6
10	Tungsten	WO_3 million tons	29.73	24.6
11	Tin	million tons of metals	18.61	30.7
12	Molybdenum	million tons of metals	89.60	24.9
13	Antimony	million tons of metals	15.18	29.1
14	Gold	thousand tons of metals	32.7	32.2
15	Silver	thousand tons of metals	726	36.1
16	Hard rock lithium	million tons of metals	5.937	36.6
	Brine lithium	million tons of metals	92.481	18.8
17	Magnesite	billion tons	13.14	19.1
18	Fluorite	million tons	953	25.7
19	Pyrite	billion tons	18.4	25.9
	Sulphurite	billion tons	0.23	60.8
20	Phosphate rock	billion tons	56	29.3
21	Potash	billion tons	2.0	40.0
22	Barite	billion tons	1.44	25.0
23	Boron	B_2O_3 million tons	189	33.5

III. Registration of Exploration and Mining Rights

1. Oil and gas

By the end of 2014, there were 1,030 oil and gas exploration rights involving a registered area of 3.93 million square kilometers, a year-on-year decrease of 3.6% and 4.9% respectively, and 705 oil and gas exploitation rights involving a registered area of 0.143 million square kilometers, a growth of 4.4% and 5.7% respectively. In the year, the Ministry of Land and Resources issued 484 oil and gas exploration permits and 36 exploitation permits.

2. Non-oil & gas minerals

In 2014, 1,269 non-oil & gas minerals exploration rights were newly approved, dropping by 4.6% and 32,600 square kilometers of newly-increased survey area were registered, dropping by 29.2%. The number of newly approved exploitation rights was 2,306, a growth of 17.6% and the newly registered exploitation area was 1,165 square kilometers, a decrease of 38.7%. The newly increased design production capacity was 0.58 billion tons per year, rising by 9.7%. In the first half year of 2015, 457 non-oil & gas minerals exploration rights were newly approved, dropping by 23.4% and 11,200 square kilometers of survey area were newly registered, dropping by 9.2%. The number of newly approved exploitation rights was 1,002, a year-on-year growth of 19.0% and the newly registered exploitation area was 984.89 square kilometers, a year-on-year increase of 48.4%. The newly increased planing production capacity was 0.255 billion tons per year, rising by 14.4% year on year.

By the end of 2014, there were 30,000 non-oil & gas minerals exploration rights in China involving a registered area of 611,500 square kilometers, a year-on-year drop of 5.2% and 9.1% respectively, and 82,000 exploitation rights involving a registered area of 104,400 square kilometers, a drop of 9.6% and 1.5% respectively (Table 2-4). The annual planing production capacity was 14.7 billion tons, basically equivalent to the previous year.

Table 2-4 Non-oil & Gas Exploration and Exploitation Rights by the End of 2014

Item	Number	Year-on-year Change (%)	Registered Area ($10^4 km^2$)	Year-on-year Change (%)
Exploration right	30480	-5.2	61.15	-9.1
Inc.: New	1269	-4.6	3.26	-29.2
Exploitation right	82450	-9.6	10.44	-1.5
Inc.: New	2306	17.6	0.1165	-38.7

Chapter III Exploration

In 2014, with the focus on the demand of resources under the new normal stage of economic development, efforts were made to continue promoting the *National Exploration and Development Planning*, through stimulation of geological exploration entities, overall deployment of various capitals and rational investment arrangement. The investment on geological exploration was RMB114.5 billion, still at a high level. The resources of major minerals, such as coal, oil, natural gas, shale gas, manganese ore, bauxite, copper, lead, zinc and gold, were increased.

I. Exploration Investment

In 2014, the exploration investment amounted to RMB114.5 billion, a year-on-year decrease of 5.4% (Figure 3-1), among which RMB19.5 billion was from the governmental investment, accounting for 17.0%; RMB95 billion from the social investment, accounting for 83.0%. The investment in geological exploration of oil and gas amounted to RMB74.3 billion, dropping by 1.2%, accounting for 64.9% of the total exploration investment. The spending on the exploration of non-oil & gas minerals was RMB 40.2 billion, a decrease of 12.5% for the

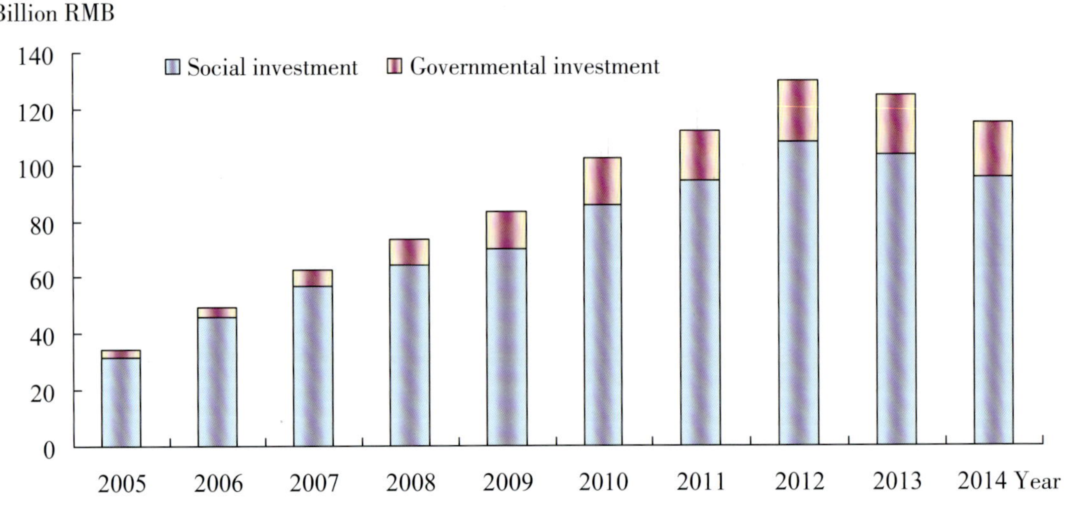

Figure 3–1 Exploration Investment

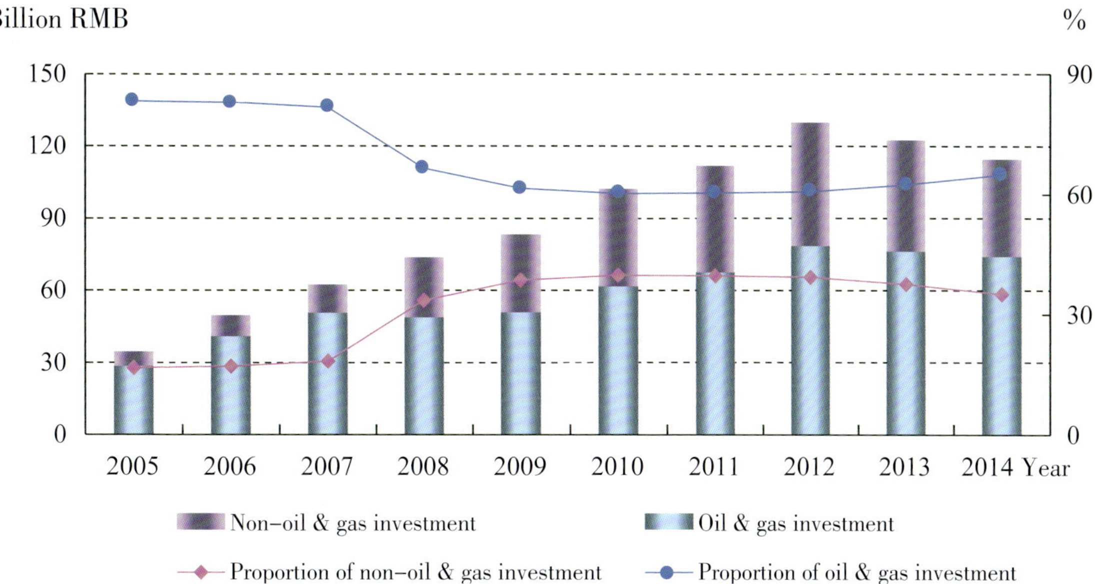

Figure 3-2 Exploration Investment of Oil & Gas and Non-Oil & Gas

second consecutive year, accounting for 35.1% (Figure 3-2), among which RMB17.9 billion was from the governmental investment, accounting for 44.5%, and RMB22.3 billion from the social investment, accounting for 55.5%.

In the year, the completed drilling was 27.41 million meters, a drop of 5.4%.

II. Energy Mineral Exploration

1. Coal

There were 17 newly-discovered large-sized ore fields in 2014. There were 2 coal orefields which newly-discovered reserves & resources surpassed 5 billion tons, including the Hongshaquan Open Coal Mine II in Black Mountain, Qitai County, Eastern Junggar Coalfield, Xinjiang and the Bayan Hada Exploration Field in Chenqi Coalfield, Inner Mongolia.

2. Conventional oil and gas

By the end of 2014, the accumulated geological reserves of oil was 36.1billion tons and natural gas 12 trillion cubic meters. In 2014, the newly-discovered reserves of oil exceeded 1 billion tons for the 8th consecutive year. There was 1 oilfield, namely Changqing Xin'anbian Oilfield of PetroChina, with the newly-discovered reserves of over 0.1 billion tons. The newly-discovered geological reserves of natural gas were over 500 billion cubic meters for the

12th consecutive year. There were 5 gas fields which newly-discovered geological reserves surpassed 100 billion cubic meters, including Changqing Shenmu Gas Field of PetroChina, Tarim Kelasu Gas Field of PetroChina, Yanchang Yan'an Gas Field in Shaanxi Province, CNOOC Zhanjiang Gas Field 17-2 of Lingshui and CNOOC Ningbo Gas Field 22-1.

3. Non-conventional oil & gas

Coal-bed methane. By the end of 2014, more than 13,000 coal-bed methane wells were drilled (over 1000 new wells in 2014, with the drilling of 1.222 million meters). In 2014, the newly-discovered geological reserves of coal-bed methane were 60.2 billion cubic meters and the accumulated geological reserves were 626.6 billion cubic meters.

Shale gas. By the end of 2014, RMB23 billion were invested in the exploration of shale gas and 780 wells drilled, with the production capacity of 1.3 billion cubic meters reached. In 2014, the newly-discovered geological reserves of shale gas were 106.8 billion cubic meters, the first submission of geological reserves since the new minerals were determined in 2011. The newly discovered shale gas field is SINOPEC Fuling .

III. Exploration of Metallic and Non-metallic Minerals

The newly increased reserves & resources of 14 minerals, including iron ore, copper, lead, zinc, bauxite, tungsten, tin, molybdenum, antimony, gold, silver, pyrite, phosphate rock and sylvite, were mainly located in Xinjiang, Yunnan, Shanxi, Inner Mongolia, Henan, Shandong, Guizhou, Jilin, Sichuan, Qinghai and Tibet in 2014. The iron ore mines with newly-discovered reserves & resources of over 0.5 billion tons included Dataigou Iron Field of Benxi city, Liaoning province and Cangshan Lanling Mine (Gulin-Lanling zone) in Shandong province. The manganese mine with the newly-discovered reserves & resources of over 0.1 billion tons was Daotuo Manganese Mine in Songtao county, Guizhou province. The newly-discovered reserves & resources of Tibet Nimu Bairong Gangjiang Copper Mine exceeded 1 million tons, those of Huaheng Danaopo Lead-Zinc Mine in Hunan province exceeded 2 million tons, those of Fengshan Fujiapo Bauxite Mine in Guangxi province exceeded 30 million tons, those of Golmud Xiarihamu HS26 Abnormal Area Copper-Nickel Mine in Qinghai province exceeded 1 million tons, those of Xinjiang Wuqia Sawayardun Gold Mine exceeded 100 tons, those of Suichang Zhedaikou Kengxi Fluorite Mine in Zhejiang province exceeded 1 million tons and those of Baokang Baishuihe Phosphate Mine in Hubei province exceeded 200 million tons.

The deep and outside exploration of the old mines resulted in outstanding economic and social benefits. Significant breakthroughs were achieved in the exploration of 14 mines, such as Qixia

Mountain Lead-Zinc Mine of Jiangsu province, Lala Copper Mine in Sichuan province and Laowan Gold Mine in Henan province, which might become large mineral deposits. Great progress has been made in 39 mines. In average, the mines life was extended by 10 years and 120,000 jobs were stabilized.

Column 3-1 Progress on Special Funds of Central Geological Exploration

In 2014, the central geological exploration funds continued driving for the National Exploration and Development Planning, survey the major minerals in state-level package exploration areas and emphasize the exploration of such national energies and urgently-needed minerals such as coal, uranium, iron, copper and potash. A batch of large and medium-sized deposits have been discovered and there are a substantial increase in the resources of coal, uranium, iron, titanium, vanadium and etc. In the year, 14 large and medium-sized ore fields have been discovered, of which 5 are large and another 5 are medium-sized.

IV. Groundwater Exploration

The land and resources departments have made efforts to survey the hydrogeological resources of the regions with severe shortage of water, such as the Wumeng Mountain area, the Taihang Mountain area, the Yimeng Mountain area and the Qaidam Basin area. In the combination of exploration and exploitation, over 170 hydrological wells were drilled, relieving the water deficiency for 300,000 local people. To support the fight against drought in Henan, Hubei and other provinces, the drilling of wells was arranged in emergency by virtue of the existing hydrogeological surveys and the catalogue of the achievements from over 1,200 hydrogeological surveys was released in time to help the professional exploration teams explore water and drill wells in the drought zones. The 1:50,000 Hydrogeological Survey Code was taken as the industrial standard and enacted. In the year, the hydrogeological survey for 1:50,000 on over 100 sheets was completed.

Chapter IV Development and Utilization of Mineral Resources

In 2014, the mining fixed assets investment increases continually, the growing rate slowed down, the lowest in the past 12 years, and its proportion in national fixed assets investments was also declining. The mining fixed assets investment of coal has a negative growth for the second consecutive year. The production of minerals keeps growing, but an obvious drop is seen in the growth. In particular, the growth also slowed down in the output of infrastructure-related raw materials, such as crude steel, ten nonferrous metals and cement. The government has issued the first evaluation index standard for comprehensive utilization of mineral resources, and made great achievements in the construction of pilot bases for comprehensive utilization.

I. Mining Fixed Assets Investment

In 2014, China's mining fixed assets investment is RMB 1.47 trillion, with an increase of 0.7%. The growth rate droped by 10.2% which is the lowest growth rate in the past 12 years. The mining fixed assets investment accounts for 2.9% of the national fixed assets investment and decreased by 0.5% compared with 3.4% in 2013. Among the mining fixed assets investment, that of coal is RMB468.2 billion, with a decrease of 9.5% and a negative growth for the second consecutive year, that of oil and gas is RMB402.3 billion, with an increase of 6.1%, that of ferrous metal is RMB169 billion, with an increase of 2.6%, that of non-ferrous is RMB163.6 billion, with an increase of 2.9%, and non-metallic mineral is RMB204.6 billion, with an increase of 13.9% (Figure 4-1).

In the first half year of 2015, China's mining fixed assets investment is RMB 526.05 billion, with a decrease of 7.7%. Among it, that of coal is RMB 168.605 billion, with a decrease of 12.8%, that of oil and gas is RMB116.895 billion, with a decrease of 6.5%, that of ferrous metal is RMB65.581 billion, with a decrease of 12.8%, that of non-ferrous is RMB62.892 billion, with a decrease of 5.7%, and non-metallic mineral is RMB92.622 billion, with an increase of 5.4%.

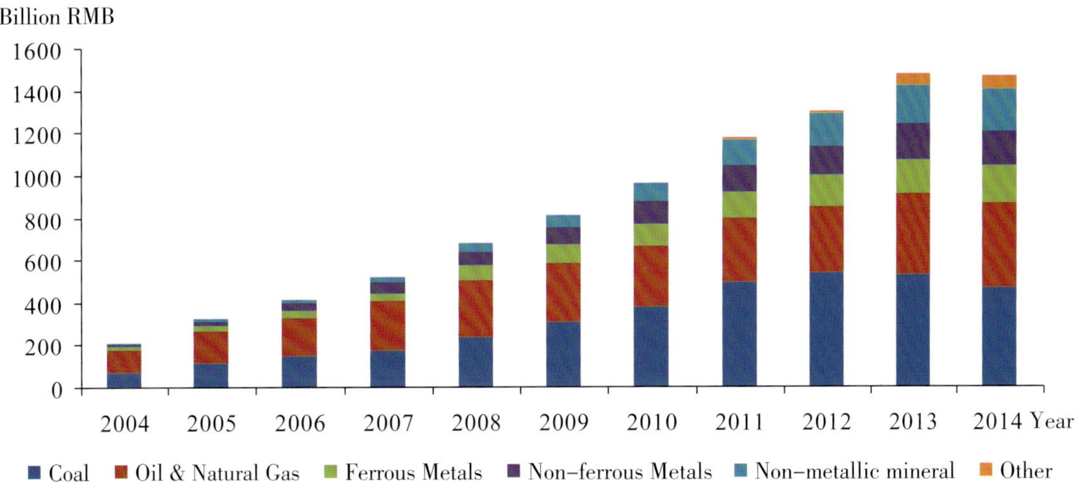

Figure 4-1 Mining Fixed Assets Investment

II. Production and Consumption

1. Energy production and consumption

China is the largest energy production and consumption country in the world. In 2014, primary energy output totals 3.60 billion tons of standard coal equivalent with an increase of 0.5% (Figure 4-2), and the consumption has increased 2.2% to 4.26 billion tons of standard coal equivalent with the self-sufficiency rate of 84.5%. China's energy structure has improved continuously, brought down the proportion of coal and increased the share of natural gas and other clean energies. The consumption structure in 2014 is as following: coal accounting for

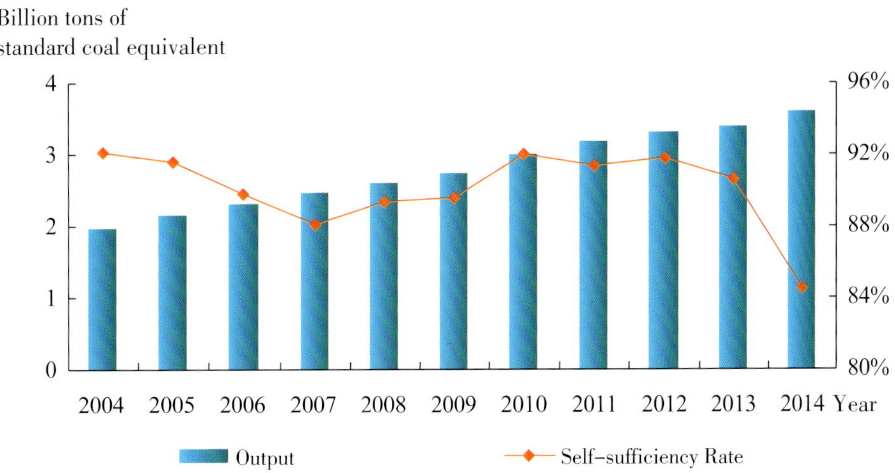

Figure 4-2 Primary Energy Production

66.0%, water power, wind power, nuclear power and natural gas jointly accounting for 16.9%.

In 2014, the coal production is 3.87 billion tons, decreased by 2.5%, ranking the first place in the world for consecutive years. 211 million tons of crude oil has been produced, with an increase of 0.7% (Figure 4-3), ranking 4th in the world. The output of natural gas is 130.16 billion cubic meters, with a growth of 7.7%, ranking 6th in the world. In the first half year of 2015, the crude oil production is 106 million tons and increased by 2.1% year-on-year, and natural gas is 63.0 billion cubic meters with an increase of 2.5%.

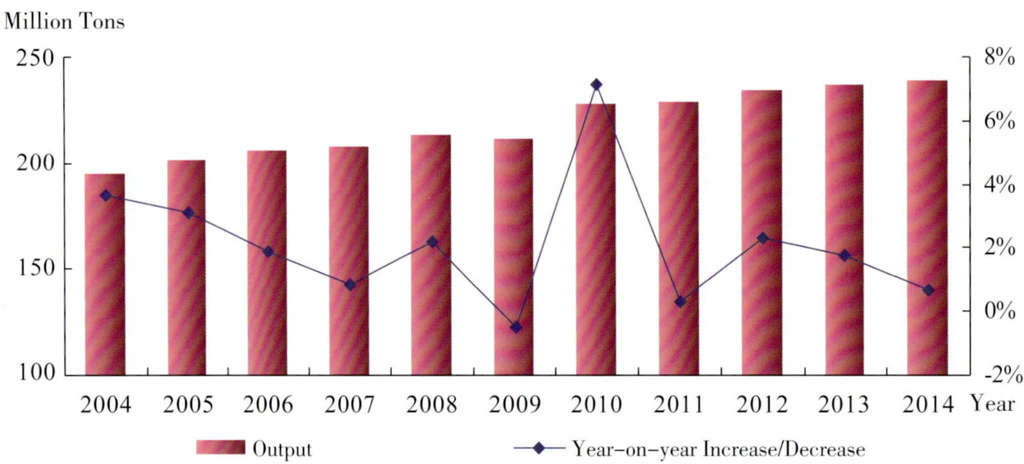

Figure 4–3 Crude Oil Production

2. Metal minerals Production and Consumption

In 2014, the output of iron ore is 1.51 billion tons, with an increase of 3.9%; crude steel 820 million tons, with an increase of 1.2% (Figure 4-4); rolled steel 1.13 billion tons, with an increase of 4.0%. The production of ten non-ferrous metals is 43.801 million tons, with an increase of 7.4%. Among them, the output of refined copper is 7.644 million tons, with an increase of 15.0% and electrolytic aluminum 27.517 million tons, with an increase of 8.2%. The output of gold is 458.1 tons, with an increase of 5.5%; the consumption is 886.09 tons, with a decrease of 24.7%. The production of crude steel, ten non-ferrous metals and gold ranks the first in the world. In the first half year of 2015, the output of iron ore amounts to 630 million tons, with a decrease of 10.7%; ten non-ferrous metals 25.263 million tons, with an increase of 9.3%; and gold 228.7 tons, with an increase of 8.4%.

3. Non–metallic minerals Production

In 2014, the output of cement is 2.48 billion tons, with a year-on-year increase of 2.3% (Figure

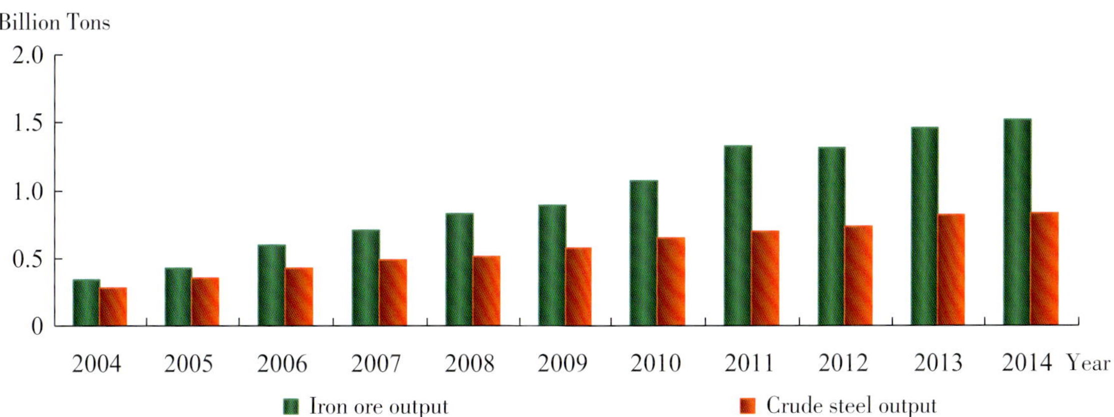

Figure 4–4 Iron Ore and Crude Steel Production

4-5); plate glass 790 million weight cases, with an increase of 1.1%; potash fertilizer 6.105 million tons (K_2O 100%), with an increase of 13.5%; and phosphate rock 120 million tons (P_2O_5 30%), with an increase of 7.0%. In the first half year of 2015, the output of cement is 1.08 billion tons, with a year-on-year decrease of 5.3%; plate glass 400 million weight cases, with a decrease of 4.2%; and phosphate rock 66.298 million tons, with an increase of 9.1%.

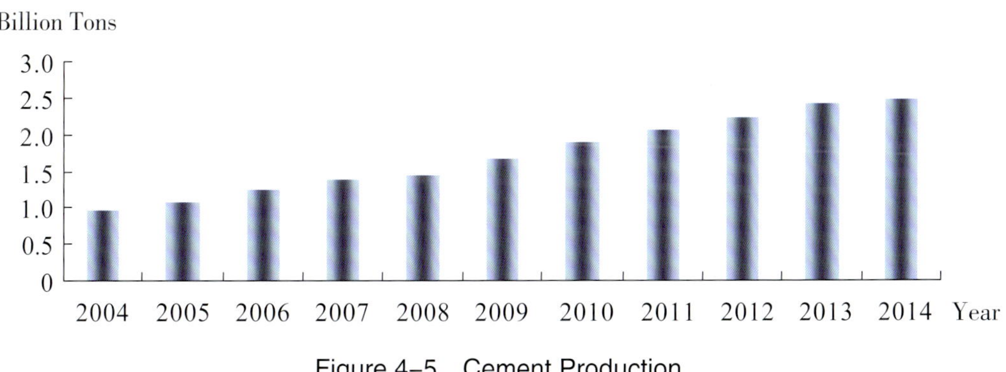

Figure 4–5 Cement Production

III. Conservation and Comprehensive Utilization

1. The comprehensive utilization standard system of minerals established

China has issued the first comprehensive utilization evaluation index standard—Technical Indexes for the Comprehensive Utilization of Mineral Resources and Their Computing Methods (DZ/T 0272-2015), stipulating the technical indexes of the comprehensive utilization and building uniform requirements for evaluating the utilization levels of mineral resources. Besides, the country has announced the third group of minimum index requirements regarding extract recovery rate, concentration recovery rate and comprehensive utilization rate for 8 minerals, such as manganese ore, chromite, bauxite, tungsten, molybdenum, pyrite, graphite and asbestos, and totally released 20 minerals of the index requirements in the past three years. Also it has formed the index system for the conservation and comprehensive utilization of mineral resources.

2. The construction of pilot bases for comprehensive utilization made in remarkable progress

The accumulated investment from the central government has reached RMB14.88 billion since the construction of pilot bases for comprehensive utilization of minerals, which has promoted an investment of RMB94.987 billion from companies. The construction has accelerated the reform and industrialization of the technologies, processes and equipments for the comprehensive utilization of 8 minerals, such as low permeable and ultra-low permeable oil and gas fields, shale gas, oil shale, vanadium titano-magnetite, solid potash, low-grade collophanite. That has made the low-grade, associated and hard-to-use resources transformed into economic recoverable resources and improved the resource guarantee capacity significantly.

3. The guidance of technology and policy enhanced

China has formulated the Directory of the Encouraged, Restricted and Eliminated Technologies for the Conservation and Comprehensive Utilization of Mineral Resources (Revised) (GTZF [2014] NO. 176), intensified the management for entrance qualification and supervised companies weeding out outdated production facilities gradually.

4. Recommended technologies promoted

In 2014, China has issued 60 recommended technologies selected from the mining industry (Table 4-1). Over the past three years, it has announced 159 recommended technologies in three batches (22 for oil and gas, 34 for coal, 70 for metal minerals and 33 for non-metallic minerals), of which there are 59 mining technologies, 40 dressing technologies and 60 technologies for the comprehensive utilization of associated minerals and tailings.

Table 4–1 Recommended Technologies for Comprehensive Utilization of Mineral Resources

10 Technologies for highly–effective mining, dressing and comprehensive utilization of coal			
1	New technique of coal slurry pipeline conveying system	2	Technique for efficient exploitation of thick coal seams under water

Continued

10 Technologies for highly-effective mining, dressing and comprehensive utilization of coal			
3	Key technique for efficient and comprehensive exploitation of ultra-thin coal seams	7	Technique for comprehensive utilization of symbiotic and associated oil shale in coal seams
4	Technique for extraction of methane gas from low-permeable coal seams	8	Technique for high-wall and steep-wall exploitation of open coal mines
5	Clean incineration and utilization technique for compound circulating fluidized bed of coal slurry	9	Technique for comprehensive utilization of abandoned heat source of mines
6	Technique for high-density, heavy-media beneficiation of high-sulfur coal refuse	10	Exploitation and upgrading technology for ultra-thin seams of open coal mines
7 technologies for highly-effective mining and comprehensive utilization of oil and gas			
11	A set of new techniques for fracturing shale gas of marine facies	15	New torch igniting system of offshore platforms and onshore terminals
12	Technique for 3D development of complicated fault-block oil reservoirs	16	Extraction technique of water injection in offshore thin-bed oil reservoirs
13	Dual horizontal well SAGD development technique for shallow ultra-viscous oil reservoirs	17	Enhanced Technique for recovery rate of air foam-driven
14	CO_2/ water alternatively driven technique for raising greatly the recovery rate of water-driven waste oil reservoirs		
29 technologies for highly-effective mining, dressing and comprehensive utilization of metals			
18	Key technique and equipment for efficient high-magnetic beneficiation of weak-magnetic ores	23	Technique for efficient exploitation by induced falling of hard-to-mine broken orebodies
19	A set of technique and equipment for dry beneficiation and tailings discarding during high-pressure grinding of magnetite	24	Technique for close-to-roof limestone curtain grouting, blocking and mining of heavy-water deposits
20	Technique for quality improvement, impurity reduction and ore dressing of Jingtieshan-type refractory iron oxide ores	25	Technique for new high-magnetic PMG for beneficiation of and integrated utilization of magnetic minerals-containing industrial residue
21	Technique of solid modeling of blasting units by sublevel caving without sill pillar	26	Technique for conversion and residual ore recovery of complex and potentially dangerous
22	Technique of producing high-purity manganese sulfate and manganese dioxide by low-grade manganese ore and sulfur-containing smoke	27	Technique for production of new wall materials by iron ore tailings

Continued

29 technologies for highly-effective mining, dressing and comprehensive utilization of metals			
28	New process for dressing of hard-to-separate micro-fine particulate iron ore	38	Technique for production of ceramic glazes and aerated concrete materials by tailings of gold mines
29	Technique for upgrading and waste reducing of metal mines by application of suspending-vibration conical-surface dressing machine	39	Key technique for high-concentration flow-regime pipeline conveying and filling of coarse aggregates of mines
30	Technique for recycle of iron minerals in tailings	40	Technique for non-driving flotation equipment of bauxite
31	Technique for fully comprehensive utilization of tailings	41	Technique for integrated recovery of valuable metals in tailings of gold mines
32	Technique for magnetic and heavy-media beneficiation of iron tailings	42	New technique for clean and efficient recovery of fine-fraction metallic minerals from tailing resources
33	Technique for low-temperature roasting and utilization of copper and cobalt containing tailings	43	Technique for integrated recovery of micro-fine particulate tungsten in tailings
34	Key technique for copper-molybdenum beneficiation of large porphyry copper-molybdenum deposits with a high content of secondary copper	44	New technique for efficient dressing of nickel and molybdenum ores with a high content of carbon,
35	Technique of dressing for complicated refractory low-grade nickel ore	45	Technique for activating flotation of sulfur concentrate from tailings of skarn-type copper mines
36	Visual dispatching management system for open pits	46	Technique for flotation separated copper from lead and zinc by liquid sulfur dioxide
37	Technique for high-magnetic beneficiation and grading of wolframite and scheelite		
14 technologies for highly-effective mining, dressing and comprehensive utilization of non-metallic ores			
47	Technique for efficient processing of calcite powder	50	Technique for extracting lithium from old brine by the adsorption method
48	Technique for production of potassium chloride by cold crystallization-direct flotation	51	Technique for gradient utilization of low-grade limestone
49	Technique for integrated governance of geological environment and landscape building of abandoned open pits	52	Technique for production of high-purity superfine torispherical silica powder and special silica new materials by konilite

Continued

14 technologies for highly-effective mining, dressing and comprehensive utilization of non-metallic ores			
53	Technique for desliming of low-grade slime-containing solid potassium ore	57	Technique for deep development of smectite products
54	Technique for purification and processing of natural vein quartz	58	Technique for safe and efficient full tailings-filling mining under the highly confined aquifer of phosphate rock
55	Technique for converting phosphogypsum into ammonium sulfate	59	New technique for comprehensive utilization of magnesium-smelting dolomite tailings
56	Technique for underground solution mining and processing of trona deposits	60	Technique for efficient recovery of machine-made fine power of gravels and cycling utilization of waste water

Chapter V Mine Ecological Environment Construction

Efforts have been intensified to fund the governance and restoration of the geological environment of mines and remarkable progress has been made in the governance and restoration of land damaged by mining development. The number of national mine parks has increased steadily and the management has been increasingly normalized. The construction of green mines has been promoted comprehensively and the construction of ecological land has been improved.

I. Geological Environment Restoration

By the end of 2014, China's spending on the governance of the geological environment of mines had amounted to RMB90.18 billion, with RMB28.73 billion from the central finance, 1,954 projects deployed and RMB61.45 billion from local finance and companies. The land damaged by mining development had covered an area of 3.03 million hectares in total, of which 810,000 hectares had been restored, with the governance rate of 26.7%. Among it, 214,000 hectares were supported by the central finance and 596,000 hectares by the local finance and companies.

The central government continued to support the geological environment restoration and demonstration projects in resource-exhausted cities. In 2014, RMB1.728 billion subsidies was allocated to govern the geological environment of mines.

By the end of 2014, the payable eash deposit for the governance and restoration of geological environment of mines was RMB159.87 billion, of which RMB86.77 billion had been paid, accounting for 54.3%. In the 99,000 mines that should make the payment throughout China, 85,900 mines had paid the eash deposit, accounting for 86.8% of the total number of mines. RMB30.74 billion was returned to the mining right holders that had performed the obligation of governance. RMB2.52 billion of the closed mines that had failed the obligation was preserved in the account.

A highlight is the construction of national mine parks. Since 2005, China has approved the construction of 72 national mine parks totally, of which 30 have been built up. In total, RMB2.29 billion has been spent on the construction of mine parks in the provinces, autonomous regions and municipalities directly under the central goverment. 41 mine parks at the provincial level have been built.

In 2014, fossil excavation was carried out in such places as Qianshan County in Anhui Province, Foshan City in Guangdong Province, Nihewan Village in Hebei Province, Lingwu City in Ningxia Hui Autonomous Region and Shanshan County in Xinjiang Uygur Autonomous Region. The excavation entities governed and restored the environment for the 930 square meters involved according to the approved recovery schemes.

II. Green Mining Development

1. Pilot construction for green mining promoted

By the end of 2014, 661 mining companies had been involved in the pilot program of national green mines construction, realizing the goal of constructing over 600 state-level pilot mines by the end of the Twelfth Five-Year Plan and playing a demonstrating and guiding role in the development of circular economy, efficient utilization of resources, guidance of green technology, ecological protection of mines and harmony and common benefits of mineral estates. In addition, the Measures on the Acceptance Inspection of State-level Green Mine Pilots (Trial Implementation) was formulated. The evaluation on the construction of the first 37 pilot entities, such as Shanxi Tongmei Datang Tashan Coal Mine, was completed, the effect and problems were summarized and suggestions on follow-up incentive policies and measures were put forward.

2. Local governments played an active role in green mine construction

Local governments have driven provincial and municipal construction of green mines orderly. Zhejiang, Hebei and Jiangxi have formulated administrative regulations and incentive policies. Inner Mongolia and Guizhou have developed implementation plans and Guangxi, Jiangxi and Beijing have drawn up construction plans.

Chapter VI Mineral Resources Management and Policies

Efforts have been made to promote the institutional reform of administrative examination and approval, accelerate the transformation of government functions and make the management of mineral resources increasingly scientific, standardized and legitimate. Since 2014, China has intensified the streamlining of administration and the delegation of power, made the market more active, modified 3 administrative regulations, promulgated 2 new regulations, cancelled 23 administrative examinations and approvals and adjusted some compensations and taxes for mineral resources.

I. Items Subject to Administrative Examination and Approval

1. 3 Administrative regulations modified

On July 29, 2014, the State Council promulgated the Decision of the State Council on Modifying Some Administrative Laws and Regulations (Order No. 653).

Modification to the Administrative Regulations for the Registration of Mineral Resources Exploration Regions: Firstly, "Regarding the exploration right that has been validated through evaluation..." as specified in Article 13.1 is changed into "Regarding the exploration right of the region which has been explored using state-funded and whose ore field has been identified, the applicants shall pay the cost of the exploration right, besides using fee of the exploration right as per Article 12"; Secondly; Article 13.2 is changed into "the cost of the exploration right formed using governmental funds should be evaluated by an agency with the qualification of assessing exploration and mining rights; the evaluation report should be registered with the competent authorities"; Thirdly Article 38 is changed into "Where the mineral resources are explored under Chinese-foreign cooperation, the Chinese party should, after signing the contract, register the contract with the original issuing authority"; Finally "Those working on regional geological survey, regional mineral resources survey, regional geophysical survey, regional geochemical survey, geological survey by aerial remote sensing, regional hydrogeological survey, regional engineering geology survey, regional environmental geology survey, marine geology survey and so on, should register with the competent administrative authorities" as specified in Article 40 is deleted.

Modification to the Administrative Regulations for the Registration of Mineral Resources Exploitation: Firstly, "Regarding the mining right that has been validated through evaluation..." as specified in Article 10.1 is changed into "To apply for the mining right of the region which has been explored using government-funded and whose ore field has been identified, the applicator should pay the cost of the mining right formed by government funds, besides using fees for the use of the mining right as specified in Article 9"; Secondly, Article 10.2 is changed into "the cost of the exploration right formed by government funds should be evaluated by an agency with the qualification of assessing exploration and mining rights; the evaluation report should be registered with the competent administrative authorities"; Finally Article 29 is changed into "The mineral resources will being exploited under Chinese-foreign cooperation, the Chinese party should, after signing the contract, register the contract with the original issuing authority".

Modification to the Administrative Regulations for the Transfer of Exploration and Mining Rights: Article 9.2 is changed into "the cost of the exploration and mining rights formed by governmental funds should be evaluated by the agencies with the corresponding qualification; the evaluation reports should be registered with the authorities in charge of exploration and mining rights registration".

2. New regulations promulgated

(1) Administrative Regulations for the Monitoring of Geological Environment

On April 29, 2014, the Administrative Regulations for the Monitoring of Geological Environment (The 59th Decree of the Ministry of Land and Resources, 2014) was promulgated in accordance with the Mineral Resources Law of the People's Republic of China, the Regulations on the Prevention and Control of Geological Disasters and other applicable laws and regulations, stipulating the purpose, basis, definition, principles, subjects, applicable scope and legal liabilities of geological environment monitoring.

(2) Regulationss on the Administrative Punishment for Land and Resources

The Regulations on the Administrative Punishment for Land and Resources (The 60th Decree of the Ministry of Land and Resources,2014) was promulgated on May 7, 2014, with the primary principles of normalizing administrative power and safeguarding the rights and interests of the masses.

3. Changes in examination and approval

(1) Twenty three examinations and approvals cancelled

Since 2014, 23 examinations and approvals relating to mineral resources have been cancelled, including examinations and approvals of distribution plans for exploration and mining rights, deployment plans or registration for exploration and mining rights, postponed collection of geological data, deployment for package exploration regions, adjustment for classification of mineral exploration risks, registration of exploration and mining rights' prices evaluation and etc. (Table 6-1)

Table 6–1 Examinations and Approvals Cancelled Since 2014

No.	Item	Category	Basis
1	Forward examination of exploration and exploitation of mineral resources under Chinese–foreign cooperation	Administrative examination and approval	Decision of the State Council on Canceling and Releasing Another Group of Administrative Examinations and Approvals (GF[2014] No. 5)
2	Registeration approval of geological survey	Administrative examination and approval	
3	Examination and approval of exploration and development of mineral resources and engineering construction in the areas beyond the relic protection zones of the national geological parks	Non–administrative examination and approval	
4	Examination and approval of distribution plans for exploration and mining rights	Non–administrative examination and approval	
5	Examination and approval of naming "Home/ City/ Land of Hot Springs"	Non–administrative examination and approval	
6	Register examination and approval of coal exploration and mining rights, in those provinces where reforming management	Non–administrative examination and approval	
7	Registration of mineral water sold in different provinces, autonomous regions and municipalities directly under the central government	Non–administrative examination and approval	Decision of the State Council on Canceling and Releasing Another Group of Administrative Examinations and Approvals (GF[2014] No. 27)

Continued

No.	Item	Category	Basis
8	Examination and approval of postponed collection of geological data	Administrative examination and approval	Decision of the State Council on Canceling and Adjusting Another Group of Administrative Examinations and Approvals (GF[2015] No. 11)
9	Examination and approval of mineral resources development and utilization in reserve regions of ore fields	Administrative examination and approval	
10	Examination and approval of consulting the geological data within the protective period by governments above the county level	Administrative examination and approval	
11	Examination and approval of plans for protecting the geological environment of mines of provinces, autonomous regions and municipalities directly under the central government	Administrative examination and approval	
12	Examination and approval of directories of places with fossils under key protection	Administrative examination and approval	
13	Examination and approval of construction of science and technology platform of the Ministry of Land and Resources	Administrative examination and approval	
14	Examination and approval of deployment for package exploration regions	Administrative examination and approval	
15	Examination and approval of adjustment of mineral exploration risk classification	Administrative examination and approval	
16	Accreditation of qualification of hydrological and water resource survey and appraisal agencies	Administrative examination and approval	
17	Examination and approval of confirming and overall plans for construction of mineral resources comprehensive utilization pilot bases	Non-administrative examination and approval	Decision of the State Council on Canceling Non-administrative Examinations and Approvals (GF[2015] No. 27)
18	Examination and approval of applications for transferring exploration and mining rights by agreements	Non-administrative examination and approval	

Continued

No.	Item	Category	Basis
19	Examination and approval of check or filing for exploration and mining rights deployment	Non-administrative examination and approval	Decision of the State Council on Canceling Non-administrative Examinations and Approvals (GF[2015] No. 27)
20	Examination and approval of the setup, alteration or cancellation of mining areas under national planning or of important value to the national economy	Non-administrative examination and approval	
21	Examination and approval of evaluation of cost of exploration and mining rights	Non-administrative examination and approval	
22	Examination and approval of overall plans for development and construction of Home/ City/ Land of Hot Springs declared by the governments of municipalities directly under the central government	Non-administrative examination and approval	
23	Examination and approval of planning for national geological parks	Non-administrative examination and approval	

(2) Retained and adjusted examinations and approvals

According to the opinions on the sorting of non-administrative examinations and approvals passed on the 91st Executive Meeting of the State Council on May 6, 2015, the non-administrative examinations and approvals of "plans for mineral resources" and "specific mineral resources under protective exploitation" have been changed into the interior management by government. The Ministry of Land and Resources has retained 9 administrative examinations and approvals, involving 19 sub-items (Table 6-2).

Table 6–2 Administrative Examinations and Approvals in Force for the Time Being

Item Code	Item Name	Sub–item	Subjects
12004	Examination and approval of mineral resources exploration	1. Registration of new exploration rights	Public institutions and enterprises
		2. Registration of extension exploration rights	Public institutions and enterprises
		3. Registration of retained exploration rights	Public institutions and enterprises

Continued

Item Code	Item Name	Sub-item	Subjects
12004	Examination and approval of mineral resources exploration	4. Registration of cancelled exploration rights	Public institutions and enterprises
		5. Registration of altered exploration rights	Public institutions and enterprises
		6. Examination and approval of pilot exploitation for the exploration of fluid minerals, such as oil and natural gas	Enterprises
		7. Examination and approval of transfer for exploration rights	Public institutions and enterprises
12005	Examination and approval of mineral resources exploitation	1. Registration of new exploitation rights	Enterprises
		2. Registration of transferred exploitation rights	Enterprises
		3. Registration of extension exploitation rights	Enterprises
		4. Delimitation of mines fields	Enterprises
		5. Registration of altered exploitation rights	Enterprises
		6. Registration of cancelled exploitation rights	Enterprises
		7. Examination and approval of schemes for protecting, controlling and restoring geological environment of mines	Enterprises
12006	Examination and approval of geological survey qualification	None	Public institutions and enterprises
12008	Registration of geological data protection	None	Public institutions and enterprises
12009	Examination and approval of Class A qualifications of geological disasters prevention and control entities	1. Examination and approval of Class A qualifications of entities that evaluate geological disaster risks	Public institutions and enterprises
		2. Examination and approval of Class A qualifications of entities that survey geological disaster-controlling projects	Public institutions and enterprises

Continued

Item Code	Item Name	Sub-item	Subjects
12009	Examination and approval of Class A qualifications of geological disasters prevention and control entities	3. Examination and approval of Class A qualifications of entities that design geological disaster-controlling projects	Public institutions and enterprises
		4. Examination and approval of Class A qualifications of entities that implement geological disaster-controlling projects	Public institutions and enterprises
		5. Examination and approval of Class A qualifications of entities that supervise geological disaster-controlling projects	Public institutions and enterprises
12010	Examination and approval of excavation of fossils under key protection	None	Public institutions, enterprises and social organizations
12011	Examination and approval of transfer, exchange and donation of the collected fossils under key protection among collection entities	None	Public institutions, enterprises and social organizations
12012	Examination and approval of fossils under key protection that entry and exit China	None	Public institutions, enterprises and social organizations
12044	Certification by the Quality Supervision and Testing Center, Ministry of Land and Resources	None	Public institutions

II. Taxes and Fees

1. Adjustment of policies

According to the Notice on Implementing the Reform of Coal Resources Tax (CS [2014] No. 72), the Notice on Adjusting the Policies of Crude Oil and Natural Gas Resources Tax (CS [2014] No. 73) and the Notice on Solving the Problems about Coal, Crude Oil and Natural Gas Charges Funds (CS [2014] No. 74) (October, 2014), released by the Ministry of Finance, mineral resources compensations rate of coal, oil and gas has dropped to zero, ad valorem has been applied to resources tax of coal, and cleanup Charges Funds associated with China since December 1, 2014. Besides, the applicable tax rate of crude oil and natural gas resources has been raised from 5% to 6%. In April, 2015, the Ministry of Finance and the National Development and Reform Commission announced jointly the Notice on Solving the Problems about the Charged Funds Involving Rare Earth, Tungsten and Molybdenum (CS [2015] No. 53), determining to bring the compensation rate for rare earth, tungsten and molybdenum ores down to zero and stop collecting price regulation funds for rare earth, tungsten and molybdenum ores from May 1, 2015 (Table 6-3 and 6-4).

Table 6-3 Compensations Rates of Mineral Resources 2015

Minerals	Rate (%)
Oil, natural gas, coal, rare earth, tungsten, molybdenum	0
Lake salt, rock salt, natural brine	0.5
Coal-bed methane, stone coal, oil sand	1
Native bitumen, oil shale; iron ore, manganese, chromite, vanadium, titanium; copper, lead, zinc, bauxite, nickel, cobalt, tin, bismuth, mercury, antimony, magnesium; bromine, arsenic	2
Uranium, thorium, terrestrial heat; niobium, tantalum, beryllium, lithium, zirconium, strontium, rubidium, cesium; germanium, gallium, indium, thallium, hafnium, rhenium, cadmium, selenium, tellurium; carbon dioxide gas, hydrogen sulfurous gas, helium gas, radon gas	3
Gold, silver, platinum, palladium, ruthenium, osmium, iridium; iron-absorbed rare earth; gemstone, jade, gem diamond; mineral water	4
Other minerals	2

Table 6-4 Items and Rates of Resources Tax Since 2014

Tax Items		Adjusted Tax Rate
I. Crude oil		6% of sales volume
II. Natural gas		6% of sales volume
III. Coal	Coking coal	2%-10% of sales volume (up to local governments)
	Others	
IV. Other non-metallic raw minerals	Ordinary	RMB0.5-20 per ton or cubic meter
	Precious	RMB 0.5-20 per kilogram or carat
V. Raw ferrous metals		RMB 2-30 per ton
VI. Raw non-ferrous metals	Rare earth ore	RMB 0.4-60 per ton
	Others	RMB 0.4-30 per ton
VII. Salt	Solid	RMB 10-60 per ton
	Liquid	RMB 2-10 per ton

2. Taxation

In 2014, China collected RMB19.737 billion compensation fees for mineral resources, a year-on-year decrease of 8.4%, and RMB108.36 billion resource taxes, an increase of 7.8%.

III. Mineral Resources Planning

1. The third round of mineral resources planning launched comprehensively

The Ministry of Land and Resources has started the third round of planning and made overall arrangement for the provincial, municipal and county planning at all levels, together with the National Development and Reform Commission, the Ministry of Finance, the Ministry of Industry and Information Technology, the Ministry of Environmental Protection and the Ministry of Commerce.

2. The top–level design for the third round of planning finished

The top-level design has been improved according to the new requirements of comprehensively deepening reform and land and resources management. The overall thinking for the third round of planning has been put forward and planning functions and major tasks for each level have been defined. The regionalized management system and the policies on differential management of minerals have been improved. Finally, arguments have been conducted on the planning targets, major items and major projects of exploration and development of mineral resources and control of geological environment of mines.

3. Local planning has been guided and promoted

The Technical Regulations for the Overall Planning of Mineral Resources at the Provincial Level and the Guiding Opinions on the Overall Planning of Mineral Resources at the Municipal Level and the County Level have been formulated to define the planning requirements for each level. At present, 31 provinces, autonomous regions and municipalities have carried out studies on the planning and arguments on major indexes and major projects and on this basis, put forward the planning guidelines at the provincial level.

IV. Management of Exploration and Mining Rights

1. The streamlining of administration has been intensified

Since 2014,10 examinations and approvals relating to the management of exploration and mining rights have been cancelled (Table 6-1).

2. Market regulation enhanced

Firstly, the "application for pausing the acceptance of new coal exploration right" has been cancelled and start new approval process of coal exploration license approval started . From September 12, 2014, when the implementation of the policy was started, to June 30, 2015, 35 exploration rights were established. Secondly, the issuance of overall exploitation control indexes for antimony has been cancelled; Thirdly, the comprehensive utilization index of tungsten has been changed from binding to guiding. Finally, "the policy of pausing the acceptance of new rare earth exploration and mining rights management" has been altered, allowing the large rare earth enterprises and groups confirmed by the state and satisfy the precondition of "overall exploitation control and the balance between exploitation and reserves" to apply for new rights of exploring and exploiting rare earth.

3. The publicity of examinations and approvals of exploration and mining rights strengthened

The information of granting and transfer of exploration and mining rights have been disclosed to the public. 14,600 pieces of basic information has been publicized in the portal web of the Ministry of Land and Resources since 2014 and 60,200 pieces accumulatively. There were 54000 pieces of exploration and mining rights registration information disclosed since 2014, and 241000 pieces from the begining.

The information on the registration of exploration and mining rights can be checked in the portal web. 134,000 checks have been made since 2014 and 386,000 accumulatively.

V. Management of Geological Survey Qualifications

1. Overview

By the end of 2014, there were 2,574 geological survey entities holding 7,336 qualifications of various types and levels, of which 2,658 were at Class A which held by 1,106 entities (including 885 state-owned entities), 2,800 were at Class B which held by 744 entities, and 1,878 were at Class C which held by 724 entities.

The qualification form by sectors : 396 were for regional geological survey, 16 for marine geological survey, 4 for oil and natural gas exploration, 660 for liquid mineral exploration, 276 for gas mineral exploration, 1,925 for solid mineral exploration, 1,028 for hydrogeology, engineering geology, environment geology survey, 773 for geophysical exploration, 364 for geochemical exploration, 5 for aerogeological survey, 84 for remote sensing geological survey, 1,344 for geological drilling (pitting) and 461 for geological experiment and testing (Figure 6-1)

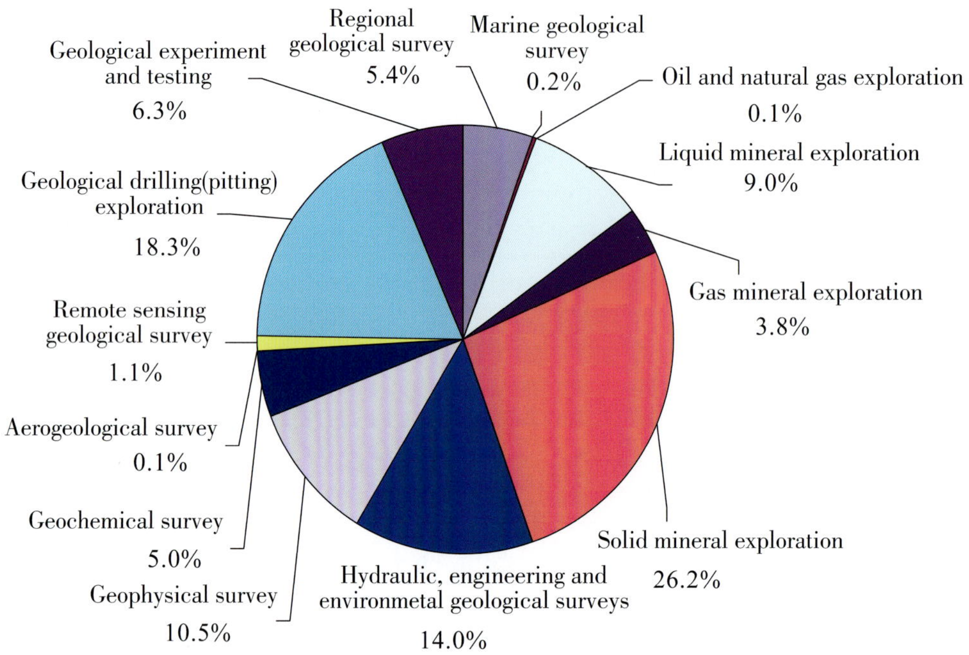

Table 6–1 Qualification Categories of Geological Survey

Based on the economic category, the foregoing geological survey entities include 1,268 state-owned entities, 21 collectively-owned entities, 12 joint-equity entities, 1,129 limited liability entities, 63 entities limited by shares, 55 private entities, 21 other entities, 1 joint venture (with funds from Chinese Taipei, Hong Kong and Macau), 1 entity with entire funds from Chinese Taipei, Hong Kong and Macau, 2 entities with entire funds from foreign countries and 1 foreign-funded shareholding company (Figure 6-2).

2. Examination and approval of geological survey qualifications

The Ministry of Land and Resources has completed the centralized acceptance, reporting and announcement of applications for establishment and renewal and the routine acceptance, examination and announcement of applications for alteration, supplementation and cancellation of geological survey qualifications for 2014, issued 389 geological survey qualification certificates(Established 196, retained 29 and altered 164), cancelled 3 qualification certificates.

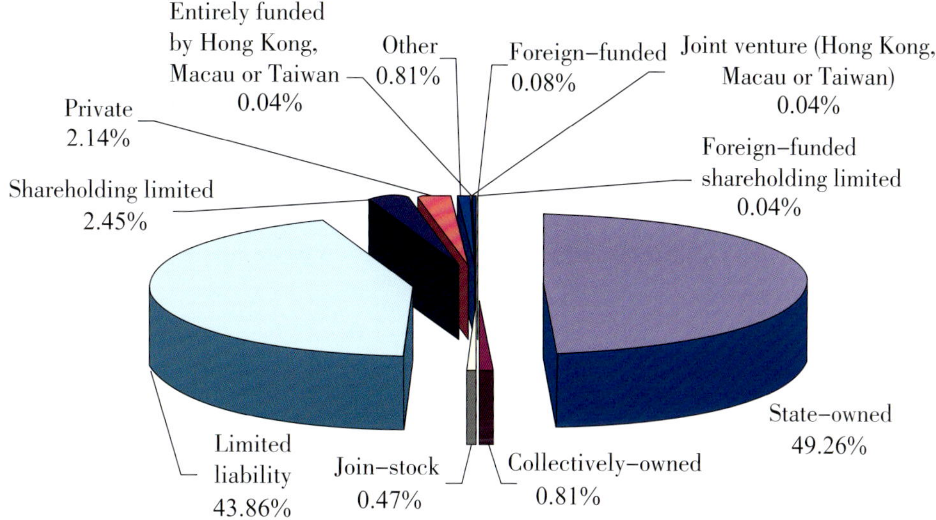

Figure 6-2 Economic Categories of Geological Survey Entities

Chapter VII
Geological Survey and Geological Data Service

In 2014, geological survey and geological data service played a more guiding and fundamental role in the economic and social development and provided important support and security for the development of economy, society and ecological civilization. The substantial achievements in geological survey have provided great support for the security of mineral resources. In addition, the collection of geological big data and the construction of the geological data sharing and service platform have been accelerated and the availability and quality of geological data service have been improved further.

I. Basic Geological Survey

1. Regional geological survey

In 2014, the regional geological survey for 1:50,000 finished 216,000 square kilometers, aggregated to 3.046 million square kilometers, accounting for 31.7% of the onshore territorial area. The regional geological revision for 1:250,000 finished 22 thousand square kilometers, aggregated to 5.935 million square kilometers, accounting for 61.7% of the onshore territorial area.

2. Regional geophysical survey

In 2014, the aeromagnetic survey for 1:50,000 finished 230 thousand square kilometers and the working level of key metallogenic belts reached to 49%. The magnetic survey, regional gravity survey and electrical method survey for 1:50,000 finished 51 thousand square kilometers, 24 thousand square kilometers and 4 thousand square kilometers respectively. The regional gravity survey for 1:250,000 finished 190 thousand square kilometers and the working level on the land rose to 59%.

3. Regional geochemical survey

In 2014, the regional geochemical exploration for 1:50,000 finished 240 thousand square kilometers and the working level of key metallogenic belts was enhanced to 35%. The regional geochemical exploration for 1:250,000 reached 51 thousand square kilometers and the working level on the land rose to 66%.

4. Remote sensing geological survey

Aerial hyperspectral data for over 2,000 square kilometers in the west of the Qilian Mountain metallogenic belt was obtained to manufacture ortho-rectification products and produce mineral information. High-precision remote sensing survey finished 5,020 square kilometers in East Kunlun, Alkin and Bangong Lake-Nujiang River metallogenic belts.

5. Marin geological survey

Efforts were continued to carry out geological surveys for 1:1,000,000 in the maritime space under the jurisdiction of China, for 1:250,000 in key maritime space and for 1:50,000 in maritime space, comprehensive geological surveys and monitoring on key costal zones, surveys on maritime oil and gas resources, exploration of natural gas hydrate (NGH) resources and other scientific ocean surveys. Among them, the filed investigation on 16 sheets under marine geological survey for 1:1,000,000 was finished. The entire maritime space under the jurisdiction of China was covered for the first time.

II. Survey and Evaluation of Mineral Resources

1. Survey and evaluation of conventional oil and gas resources

A series of significant achievements have been obtained in comprehensive research, overall evaluation and multi-function survey of oil and gas basins, with a focus on new areas, new series of strata, new types and new cognition.

The new area survey opened up new fields. 3 lithologic traps were discovered in the on-site seismic exploration of Tibet Lunpola Basin, providing strategic reserves for the oil and gas exploration in the Qiangtang Basin. Besides, brown crude oil was discovered in the Muli Area in the northeast of Southern Qilian Basin, leading to a bright prospect for the multi-energy exploration.

A group of new targets were identified in the survey of new series of strata. Light crude oil was obtained in "Tushen 1" well in the peripheral Tuquan area of Songliao Basin. Important breakthroughs were made in the Middle-Lower Jurassic in the northeast. Oil and gas-containing rock layer was discovered in the Permian System in the Bogda Region in the south rim of

Junggar Basin. All of these started a new field of oil and gas exploration.

Significant new knowledge was obtained in basic geological survey. 9 important blocks were selected in the Qiangtang Basin, and 6 important favorable blocks were outlined in the carbonatite oil and gas survey in the large basins of Western China. Follow-up explorations verify that great progress has been made in the Midwest Triassic System of Sichuan Basin, the Ordovician System of Erdos Basin and the Lower Cambrian System of Tazhong Area, oil and gas bidding blocks were selected and the Xinjiang oil and gas system reform was supported enormously.

2. Survey and evaluation of non–conventional oil & gas resources

In the survey of coal-bed methane, 28 basin groups and 56 favorable zones were selected. High-quality oil shale was discovered in the peripheral of Songliao Basin and thick-layer oil sand was acquired in the Weibei Upheaval of South Erdos Basin.

Substantial progress was made in the survey of shale gas in the marine facies of South China. Analysis proved a higher content of shale gas in Niutitang Formation of Northwest Hunan Province and Dawuba Formation in South Guizhou Province. The survey of shale gas in North China expanded the new areas of the transitional facies of land and sea. Shale bed with a higher content of gas was discovered in the Yanchang Formation of South Erdos Basin. Gas exploration abnormities were discovered in "Weishen-1" well in Henan Province. Comprehensive survey and evaluation selected 42 favorable blocks, providing basis for the invitation for bids of shale gas blocks.

3. Survey and evaluation of uranium resources

By the end of 2014, the metallogenic prospects of uranium-bearing sandstone in 13 basins, such as the Ili Basin and the Erdos Basin, and the peripheral resources potential of key uranium mineralizing zones, such as South Momoyama-Chu-kuang Mountains, Gan-Hang Belt and Xuefeng Mountain-Motianling, were evaluated in a systematic way and the uranium survey exceeded 600 thousand square kilometers. Over 500 coal exploration fields were screened and over 30 thousand coalfields and oil drillings were checked. 1,500 potential uranium resource drillings or so were discovered. There were 1,400 potential mineralized holes, over 200 prospecting targets and over 20 newly-discovered ore fields and occurrences.

4. Survey and evaluation of geothermal resources

The survey and evaluation of shallow geothermal resources of 256 prefecture-level cities and the survey and division of geothermal resources of 31 provinces, districts and cities were completed comprehensively. 215°C terrestrial heat was obtained at the depth of 230 meters in Gudui Town, Cuomei County, Tibet, showing a promising prospect of resources. 150°C hot dry rock was discovered at the depth of 3,050 meters in Guide County, Qinghai Province.

5. Survey and evaluation of non–energy mineral resources

The mineral geological survey for 1:50,000 finished 50 thousand square kilometers. 6,300 geochemical and geophysical exploration abnormities were determined, over 1,000 mineral occurrences or mineralized spot were discovered, over 300 prospecting targets were outlined and 35 ore fields were newly discovered. A super large copper-gold-iron polymetallic ore zone was discovered in the Gaize Shelama Region, Tibet. A large prospecting copper-nickel ore deposit was discovered in the north piedmont of East Tianshan Mountain of Xinjiang. A large gold mineralization belt was discovered in the Yazhaqu Region of East Kunlun of Qinghai Province. A super large gold ore prospect was proved in the periphery of Hunan Dawan Gold Mine. 200 thousand tons prospecting tin ore was discovered in Shixing County, Guangdong Province. 2 million tons of chromite resources were reported in South Luobusha Town, Tibet. Chromite ore was discovered newly and estimated 250 thousand tons in the Xiangka Mountain ore field in Tibet, which might become a 10-million-ton resource base. 100 million tons of prospecting potassium chloride resources was increased in Qaidam Basin, Qinghai Province. 640 thousand tons of lithium oxide resources (super-large size) were increased in the periphery of Jiajika Region, Sichuan Province. 18 high-purity quartz veins were discovered in Chengbu County, Hunan Province, with a SiO_2 content of over 99%. 2 medium-sized crystalloid graphite ore fields were newly discovered in Yichang City, Hubei Province and nearly 1 million tons of prospecting colombite mineralizing belt was discovered newly in Zhuxi County, Hubei Province.

III. Geological Data Management and Service

1. The supervision over the collection intensified

(1) More resultant geological data collected increasingly

In 2014, 14,827 pieces of geological data were collected throughout China, of which the data on mineral geology and hydrological-engineering-environmental geology accounted for 42.8% and 47.4% respectively, and the data on oil and gas amounted to 604 pieces, an increase of 17.7% over the previous year. By the end of 2014, the number of pieces of geological data collection institutions at the ministerial level and the provincial level had reached 459.5

thousand, rising by 3.7%.

(2) The collection of original geological data grown steadily

In 2014, the geological data collection institutions at the ministerial level and the provincial level received 2,062 pieces of original geological data totally, an increase of 78% over the previous year. The entrusted oil and gas data preservation institutions received 191.9 thousand pieces of original geological data. By the end of 2014, the amount of original geological data under entrusted preservation had reached nearly 600 thousands, rising by 17%.

(3) Collection of geological material data enriched constantly

35 types of geological material data from mineral geological survey and regional geological survey have been collected. The Cores and Samples Center of Land and Resources has preserved such geological material data as 298,200 meters of rock cores and 40,814 slices of 557 drillings. In 2014, the entrusted oil, gas and other geological material preservation institutions received 89.9 thousand meters of rock cores and 250.7 thousand bags of rock debris and accepted the entrusted preservation of 194 thousand meters of rock core and 3 million bags of rock debris.

(4) Online supervision launched comprehensively

By the end of 2014, over 200 thousand pieces of data on exploration and mining rights and geological projects as well as over 70 thsoudand kinds of collected achievements, original geological data and geological material data had been collected in the nationwide geological data collection supervision platform.

2. Remarkable achievements in the socialized service

(1) Outstanding progress in the information sharing and service platform

In 2014, 34 nodes for the geological data collection departments of the provincial, district and municipal land and resources authorities and the Information Center of the Ministry of Land and Resources, China Geological Survey Development and Research Center (National Geological Archives of China) and the Cores and Samples Center of Land and Resources were built up completely, the system of "scattered preservation and network service" was established basically and non-confidential geological data service was provided to the whole society.

In the year 2014, the geological data sharing and service platform received nearly 620 thousand views and directory services of 358 thousand pieces of data was provided, an increase of 19 thousand over the previous year.

(2) Social service improved further

In 2014, China Geological Survey Development and Research Center (National Geological Archives of China) and the geological data collection departments of 31 provinces, districts and municipalities provided on-site services for 25.5 thousand person-times and 101 thousand data services; the Cores and Samples Center of Land and resources provided on-site services for 5,646 person-times; the entrusted oil, gas and other geological data preservation entities provided on-site services for 8,321 person-times and 26.6 thousand original geological data services.

(3) Service products enriched constantly

In 2014, the services of 1:50,000 mineral resources survey results for 2,565 sheets were provided to the society; basic information of 900 thousand geological drillings and bar chart information of 50 thousand drillings were released via the national key geological drilling service platform; serial map data of hydrological-engineering-environmental geology surveys for 1:50,000, data on the geological documents of 109 package exploration areas, Geological Atlas of Land, Resources and Environment of Beijing-Tianjin-Hebei Region and China Atlas of Natural Resources were issued to the public.

(4) Digital service products increased significantly

The geological data collection departments at the ministerial level and the provincial level have given great impetus to the digital service of geological data. Among the data collected, there has been 404.9 thousand pieces of electronic archives, accounting for 88.1%. 15 provinces, districts and municipalities, such as Tianjin and Hebei, have digitalized all of their geological data, which has provided powerful support for the construction of the sharing and service platforms and e-reading rooms and promoted the reading and utilization of electronic data. In 2014, the electronic data were copied for 38,700 times in the collection departments at the ministerial level and the provincial level.

Chapter VIII Scientific and Technological Innovation and International Cooperation

Positive progress has been made in the scientific and technological innovation and international cooperation pertaining to mineral resources since 2014. New generation of stratigraphic chart has been released formally and a group of new geological exploration equipments have been developed. 12 national standards and 75 voluntary industrial standards for geology and mineral resources have been promulgated, enhancing the support for the exploration, development and management of mineral resources. Besides, several international mineral conferences, such as the Fifth APEC Ministers Responsible for Mining Meeting, have been held successfully, deepening the bilateral and multi-lateral cooperation and exchanges in respect of geology and mineral resources.

I. Basic Geological and Mineral Theoretical Research

1. New generation of stratigraphic chart released formally

The Stratigraphic Chart of China 2014 and the 2014 Stratigraphic Guide of China and Its Specifications have been revised on the basis of Version 2001, fully showing the country's stratigraphic research achievements for the past decades and referring to the latest international progress in stratigraphic studies. Both have been published under the approval of the Ministry of Land and Resources (GTZ [2014] No. 374).

2. The oldest Asian zircon discovered in the Longquan Region of Cathaysia Massif

Two zircon fragments of Priscoan have been discovered for the first time in the mica-quartz schist in the Longquan Terrain of Cathaysia Massif. One of them is aged 4.127 billion years, the oldest one in Asia.

3. Crustal structure and evolutionary process of the ancient continent of North China revealed

Zircon fragments formed 3.8 to 3.5 billion years ago were discovered in East Hebei Province and 3.8 to 3.1-bilion-year multi-stage magmatic activities were discovered in Anshan Area, proving the Ordos Massif drawn violently into the tectonic-heating event in late paleoproterozoic era, marking off three ancient continental blocks aged over 2.6 billion years in North China Craton and improving the understanding of the early crustal evolution, crust-mantle interaction and sedimentary metamorphic iron in the same period of time.

4. Major achievements obtained in the studies on the abstriction of Wenchuan Earthquake

The data on the rapid agglutination of the fracture caused by an earthquake was recorded for the first time, improving the facture theories and being of great significance for understanding the triggering of Wenchuan Earthquake.

II. Techniques of Mineral Exploration, Exploitation and Utilization

1. A group of new geological exploration equipments developed

A group of deep-ocean unmanned remote-control working system (called "Sea Horse" for short) with a localization rate of 90% have been developed and tested at the depth of 4,502 meters in South China Sea. The principled prototype for ZSM-6 electronic gravimeter has been developed, and intelligent completely. The development of TOF-SIMS scientific instruments specific to isotope geology has succeeded and a group of multiple-reflection mass analyzers have been designed, realizing the preliminary focusing of primary ions on the surface of samples and the pulse attack of ion beams on samples and detecting the signal of secondary ions. Furthermore, internationally advanced Φ2000 full-circle-swinging casting drillers have been developed, reaching a record drilling depth of gravel deposits.

2. The methods and techniques system for geological exploration improved further

A multiple-function airborne geophysical exploration data processing system with proprietary intellectual property rights has been developed (GeoProbe Mager). The techniques and methods for marine geochemical survey have been improved, supporting analytical schemes for the analysis on geochemical constituents of offshore sediments formulated and a series of supporting technologies and methods established. Besides, key techniques of UAV reliability, real-time delivery of big data, communication link relaying of mountainous areas and rapid processing of data have been mastered and a UAV remote-sensing emergency monitoring technology system has been built up preliminarily.

3. Application demonstration has promoted effectively the utilization of technologies and equipments

The UAV geophysical exploration system has been improved to the applicable level. Solid prospecting demonstration of the great-depth three-dimensional exploration system has succeeded.

4. Comprehensive utilization techniques applied better

Great progress has been made in the development and industrialization of the new process of "flotation, cluster and concentrated magnetic separation" of rare earth ore. Major breakthroughs have been achieved in the low-grade bauxite dressing technology in Yunnan-Chongqing Region. New types of sulfur flotation foaming agent and activating agent have been researched and developed, improving the selectivity of sulfur flotation and realizing the efficient utilization of sulfur in bauxite.

III. Technical Standards for Geology and Mineral Resources

China has implemented 12 national standards (Table 8-1), such as Methods for Chemical Analysis of Copper Ores, Lead Ores and Zinc Ores, and recommended 75 industrial standards pertaining to geology and mineral resources, such as Regulation of Shale Gas Resources/ Reserves Estimation, further improving the technical standards' support for the exploration, development and management of mineral resources.

Table 8-1 Related National Standards Promulgated Since 2014

National Standard Code	National Standard Name
GB/T 16950-2014	Geological Core Drilling Tools
GB/T 30712-2014	Provision of Permissible Errors for Measurement of Polished Diamond Mass
GB/T 30713-2014	Microscopic Method of Ink Stone Identification
GB/T 30714-2014	Determination of Rare Earth in Ink-stone by Inductively Coupled Plasma Mass Spectrometry
GB/T 14353.13-2014	Methods for Chemical Analysis of Copper Ores, Lead Ores and Zinc Ores—Part 13: Determination of Gallium Content, Indium Content, Thallium Content, Tungsten Content and Molybdenum Content

Continued

National Standard Code	National Standard Name
GB/T 14353.14-2014	Methods for Chemical Analysis of Copper Ores, Lead Ores and Zinc Ores—Part 14: Determination of Germanium Content
GB/T 14353.15-2014	Methods for Chemical Analysis of Copper Ores, Lead Ores and Zinc Ores—Part 15: Determination of Selenium Content
GB/T 14353.17-2014	Methods for Chemical Analysis of Copper Ores, Lead Ores and Zinc Ores—Part 17: Determination of Thallium Content
GB/T 14353.18-2014	Methods for Chemical Analysis of Copper Ores, Lead Ores and Zinc Ores—Part 18: Determination of Copper Content, Lead Content, Zinc Content, Cobalt Content and Nickel Content
GB/T 958-2015	Geological Legends Used for Regional Geological Maps
GB/T3 1390 -2015	Appraisal for View Stone
GB/T3 1432-2015	Dushan Yu—Denomination and Classification

IV. International Cooperation

1. International cooperation in mining industry expanded

Firstly, the Fifth APEC Ministers Responsible for Mining Meeting, China Mining Congress and Expo 2014, 2014 China-ASEAN Mining Cooperation Forum and China (Changsha) Mineral & Gem Show were held successfully. Secondly, the mining cooperation with the U.S., Argentina, Chile and Mexico has been included in the general framework of bilateral cooperation. The cooperation with the U.S. regarding the exploration and exploitation of shale gas has been strengthened and China-U.S. Forum on the Sustainable Development of Unconventional Oil and Gas Resources was held jointly. Besides, the 4th meeting of China-Mexico Mining Cooperation Workgroup was held. Thirdly, the cooperation with such conventional mining giants as Canada, Australia, Russia and South Africa has been consolidated and achievements have been obtained in improving inter-ministerial dialogue and cooperation mechanisms, propelling the cooperation in mining investment and trading and strengthening scientific, technological and information exchanges. Finally, the cooperation with such new economies as Central Asia, Southeast Asia, Latin America and Africa has been expanded. And cooperative intentions have been reached regarding the cooperation in shale gas development and utilization, geochemical survey and geological data sharing with Uzbekistan, Kazakhstan, Indonesia, Poland and other countries.

2. International cooperation in science and technology has been enhanced.

Firstly, active efforts have been made to promote the establishment of the UNESCO Global-Scale International Geochemical Research Center in the Institute of Geophysical and Geochemical Exploration of Chinese Academy of Geological Sciences as well as the proposed plan of "Providing resources for our descendants". Secondly, the 3rd World Landslide Forum, the 8th International Conference on Salt Lake Research and other major international congresses have been hosted, improving the international influence of China's geosciences. Finally, China-SCO Geosciences Cooperation Research Center has been founded, offering an important platform for SCO member states to improve their cooperation in geosciences.

2015

中国矿产资源报告

China Mineral Resources

中华人民共和国国土资源部　编

地质出版社

·北　京·

图书在版编目（CIP）数据

中国矿产资源报告．2015 / 中华人民共和国国土资源部编．—北京：地质出版社，2015. 10

ISBN 978-7-116-09440-6

Ⅰ. ①中… Ⅱ. ①中… Ⅲ. ①矿产资源－研究报告－中国－2015 Ⅳ. ① F426.1

中国版本图书馆 CIP 数据核字（2015）第 235892 号

Zhongguo Kuangchan Ziyuan Baogao 2015

责任编辑：祁向雷　田　野

责任校对：李　玫

出版发行：地质出版社

社址邮编：北京海淀区学院路 31 号，100083

电　　话：(010) 66554528 (邮购部)；(010) 66554692 (编辑室)

网　　址：http://www.gph.com.cn

传　　真：(010) 66554686

印　　刷：北京地大天成印务有限公司

开　　本：889mm × 1194mm　1/16

印　　张：6.25

字　　数：180千字

印　　数：1—2000册

版　　次：2015年10月北京第1版

印　　次：2015年10月北京第1次印刷

定　　价：58.00

书　　号：978-7-116-09440-6

（如对本书有建议或意见，敬请致电本社；如本书有印装问题，本社负责调换）

编　委　会

前言

2014年，中国政府继续实施找矿突破战略行动，地质找矿成果显著，主要矿产查明资源储量增长明显，矿产资源基础进一步夯实。主要矿产品生产与进口持续增长，供应能力进一步加强。加快推进地质矿产调查评价工作，地质工作对经济社会的服务水平进一步提高。促进生态文明建设，加强矿山地质环境治理恢复工作，矿山开发损毁土地治理率超过四分之一。

中国政府进一步简政放权，多措并举激发市场活力，矿产资源管理更加规范有序，节约与综合利用取得新进展。2014年以来政府取消了23项涉及地质矿产类的审批事项，将煤炭、石油、天然气等矿产资源补偿费费率降为零，煤炭资源税实行从价定率计征。发布首个矿产资源综合利用指标标准和8个矿种的开采回采率、选矿回收率、综合利用率最低指标要求，有力地推动矿产资源节约与综合利用。

为使社会公众更好地掌握中国矿产资源勘查与开发利用状况，更全面地了解矿产资源管理政策，同时也为了切实增强国土资源部门公共服务能力，推进政务信息公开，国土资源部从2011年起组织编制《中国矿产资源报告》。本年度报告系统分析了矿产资源形势，着重介绍了2014年以来中国在矿产资源勘查和开发利用、矿山生态环境建设、地质矿产调查评价等方面的主要进展，从矿产资源规划、矿业权、储量、勘查和监管等方面阐述矿产资源管理动态，从矿产资源政策法规体系建设、税费制度等方面阐述改革进展和政策要点，从地质理论、矿产资源勘查和开发利用技术等方面展示中国地质矿产科技创新的最新成果，并简要介绍了矿产资源领域国际合作状况。

希望本报告能成为国内外广大关心和支持中国矿产资源事业发展的人士了解和把握中国矿产资源总体状况的重要窗口。

本报告统计数据主要来源于中华人民共和国国家统计局、中华人民共和国国土资源部和中华人民共和国海关总署，未包括香港特别行政区、澳门特别行政区和台湾省的统计数据。

目　录

第一章　矿产资源形势 …… 1

第二章　矿产资源状况 …… 3

一、查明资源储量 …… 3

二、矿产资源潜力 …… 6

三、矿业权登记 …… 7

第三章　矿产资源勘查 …… 9

一、地质勘查投入 …… 9

二、能源矿产勘查 …… 9

三、金属与非金属矿产勘查 …… 11

四、地下水资源勘查 …… 11

第四章　矿产资源开发利用 …… 13

一、采矿业固定资产投资 …… 13

二、矿产品生产与消费 …… 14

三、矿产资源节约与综合利用 …… 16

第五章　矿山生态环境建设 …… 19

一、矿山地质环境治理恢复 …… 19

二、绿色矿业发展 …… 19

第六章　矿产资源管理与政策 …… 21

一、矿产资源管理制度变化 …… 21

二、矿产资源税费 …… 25

三、矿产资源规划 …… 26

四、矿业权管理 …… 27
五、地质勘查资质管理 …… 27
第七章　地质矿产调查评价与地质资料服务 …… 30
一、基础地质调查 …… 30
二、矿产资源调查评价 …… 31
三、地质资料管理与服务 …… 32
第八章　科技创新与国际合作 …… 35
一、基础地质与矿产理论研究 …… 35
二、矿产资源勘查开发技术 …… 36
三、地质矿产技术标准 …… 36
四、国际合作 …… 37

第一章　矿产资源形势

2014年以来，全球矿业伴随世界经济调整而持续低迷，全球矿产品需求疲软。与此同时，中国矿业发展进入调整期。为了促进矿业发展，中国政府通过加强矿产资源勘查、提升矿产资源节约与综合利用水平、加大简政放权力度、提高社会服务水平等措施激发矿业市场活力，促进矿业转型升级。

进一步摸清家底。2014年，地质勘查投入1145亿元，新发现大中型矿产地249处。油气勘查取得重大突破，页岩气首次探明地质储量1068亿立方米，石油勘查新增探明地质储量10.6亿吨，天然气9438亿立方米。45种主要矿产中有36种矿产的查明资源储量增长，其中石油剩余技术可采储量增长2.0%，天然气增长6.5%；煤炭查明资源储量增长3.2%，铁矿增长5.6%，铜矿增长6.3%，铝土矿增长3.2%，金矿增长9.4%。新的油气资源动态评价显示，中国石油地质资源量1085亿吨，常规天然气68万亿立方米，页岩气134万亿立方米，煤层气36.8万亿立方米。25种重要矿产资源潜力评价表明，矿产资源平均查明率为30.3%，找矿潜力巨大。2000米以浅，煤炭预测资源量3.88万亿吨，资源查明率为29.6%；铁矿预测资源量1960亿吨，资源查明率为33.1%；铜矿预测资源量3.04亿吨，资源查明率为29.5%；铝土矿预测资源量179.7亿吨，资源查明率为20.3%。

加强资源节约与综合利用。2014年，中国一次能源、粗钢、十种有色金属、黄金产量均位居全球首位。其中，一次能源生产总量为36.0亿吨标准煤，原煤产量38.7亿吨，原油产量2.11亿吨，天然气产量1301.6亿立方米；一次能源消费总量为42.6亿吨标准煤，能源自给率为84.5%。生产粗钢8.2亿吨，十种有色金属4380.1万吨，黄金458.1吨。2014年，中国矿产品贸易总额为1.09万亿美元，同比增长5.7%。其中，进口煤炭2.91亿吨，下降10.9%；石油3.38亿吨，增长5.1%；铁矿石9.33亿吨，增长13.8%。制订和发布了矿产资源综合利用评价指标标准，连续三年共发布20个矿种的开采回采率、选矿回收率、综合利用率指标要求，主要矿种的矿产资源节约与综合利用评价指标体系初步形成。连续三年共优选出159项先进适用技术予以推广，推动矿产资源综合利用示范基地建设、资源枯竭型城市矿山地质环境治理工程和矿山地质环境治理示范工程，分四批优选661家矿山企业作为国家级绿色矿山试点单位。

完善矿产资源管理政策。中国政府对矿产资源勘查区块登记、开采登记和探矿权采矿权转让管理等行政法规进行了修改，发布了地质环境监测管理办法和国土资源行政处罚办法，取消了23项与矿产资源相关的行政及非行政审批事项。将煤炭、原油、天然气等矿产资源补偿费降为零费率，煤炭资源税实行从价定率计征。

提高地质工作服务水平。截至2014年底，1 ∶ 5万区域地质调查和1 ∶ 25万区域地质修测面积分别占陆域国土面积的31.7%和61.7%。首次实现中国管辖海域1 ∶ 100万区域地质调查全覆盖。2014年，施工探采结合水文井170多眼，解决了30万缺水群众饮水困难。全国地质资料共享服务平台全年访问量62万次；国家和省级地质资料机构提供资料服务13万份次。国土资源实物地质资料中心共接待服务5646人次。

中国经济发展进入“新常态”，GDP进入中高速增长阶段，对大宗矿产保持较高的需求，对高新技术产业相关的矿产资源需求快速增长。同时，生态文明建设对矿产资源勘查开发提出了新要求。因此，地质工作需要转型升级，矿产资源管理需要主动适应形势变化，不断深化矿产资源管理制度改革，着重发挥科技支撑作用，切实提高成果资料的服务水平。

第二章　矿产资源状况

2014年，煤炭、石油、天然气、页岩气、锰矿、铝土矿、金矿、钨矿、钼矿和磷矿等重要矿产勘查新增查明资源储量增长明显，其中页岩气首次探获地质储量。25种矿产资源潜力评价工作全面完成，结果表明中国找矿潜力巨大。

一、查明资源储量

1. 查明资源储量变化

2014年，45种主要矿产的查明资源储量有36种增长，5种减少，4种没有变化，其中页岩气首次探获地质储量。能源和黑色金属矿产查明资源储量普遍增长，石油剩余技术可采储量同比增长2.0%，天然气增长6.5%，煤炭查明资源储量增长3.2%，铁矿增长5.6%，锰矿增长18.5%；除锡矿外，有色金属矿产查明资源储量均有不同程度增长，其中铜矿增长6.3%，镍矿增长12.9%，铅矿增长9.6%；贵金属矿产中，金矿增长9.4%，银矿增长6.3%；多数非金属矿产查明资源储量有所增长，石膏和钾盐增长明显，而重晶石和硅藻土有所下降（表2-1）。

表2-1　45种主要矿产查明资源储量

矿产名称	单位	2013年	2014年	增减变化/%
煤　炭	亿吨	14842.9	15317.0	3.2
石　油	亿吨	33.7	34.3	2.0
天然气	亿立方米	46428.8	49451.8	6.5
页岩气	亿立方米	–	254.6	–
铁　矿	矿石 亿吨	798.5	843.4	5.6
锰　矿	矿石 亿吨	10.3	12.2	18.5
铬铁矿	矿石 万吨	1142.0	1162.0	1.8
钒　矿	V_2O_5 万吨	5713.4	6074.5	6.3
钛　矿	TiO_2 亿吨	7.6	7.62	0.9
铜　矿	金属 万吨	9111.9	9689.6	6.3
铅　矿	金属 万吨	6737.2	7384.9	9.6

续表

矿产名称	单位	2013年	2014年	增减变化/%
锌　矿	金属 万吨	13737.7	14486.1	5.5
铝土矿	矿石 亿吨	40.2	41.5	3.2
镍　矿	金属 万吨	901.1	1016.9	12.9
钴　矿	金属 万吨	63.7	67.0	5.3
钨　矿	WO_3 万吨	701.4	720.5	2.7
锡　矿	金属 万吨	425.5	418.9	-1.6
钼　矿	金属 万吨	2620.2	2826.0	7.9
锑　矿	金属 万吨	262.9	284.0	8.0
金　矿	金属 吨	8974.7	9816.0	9.4
银　矿	金属 万吨	22.3	23.7	6.3
铂族金属	金属 吨	372.4	372.3	-0.04
锶　矿	天青石 万吨	4566.5	4566.5	0.0
菱镁矿	矿石 亿吨	28.9	29.1	0.7
萤　石	矿物 亿吨	2.11	2.23	5.7
耐火粘土	矿石 亿吨	25.1	25.2	0.5
硫铁矿	矿石 亿吨	56.9	58.3	2.4
磷　矿	矿石 亿吨	205.7	214.5	4.3
钾　盐	KCl 亿吨	10.1	11.2	11.3
硼　矿	B_2O_3 万吨	7613.6	7622.5	0.1
芒　硝	Na_2SO_4 亿吨	1113.0	1170.9	5.2
重晶石	矿石 亿吨	3.12	3.05	-2.2
水泥用灰岩	矿石 亿吨	1198.8	1235.1	3.0
玻璃硅质原料	矿石 亿吨	73.4	75.8	3.3
石　膏	矿石 亿吨	850.4	1007.2	18.4
高岭土	矿石 亿吨	25.0	26.7	6.5
膨润土	矿石 亿吨	28.0	28.7	2.7
硅藻土	矿石 亿吨	4.7	4.5	-3.9
饰面花岗岩	亿立方米	25.9	26.7	3.2
饰面大理岩	亿立方米	15.1	15.6	3.4
金刚石	矿物 千克	3396.5	3396.5	0.0
晶质石墨	矿物 亿吨	2.2	2.2	0.0

续表

矿产名称	单 位	2013年	2014年	增减变化/%
石　棉	矿物 万吨	9072.4	9164.6	1.0
滑　石	矿石 亿吨	2.77	2.76	−0.4
硅灰石	矿石 亿吨	1.60	1.60	0.0

注：石油、天然气、页岩气为剩余技术可采储量。

- 表示无统计数据

2. 勘查新增查明资源储量

2014 年，重要矿产均有勘查新增查明资源储量。石油勘查新增探明技术可采储量 1.9 亿吨，天然气 4749.6 亿立方米，页岩气 266.9 亿立方米。煤炭勘查新增查明资源储量 561 亿吨，铁矿 43.0 亿吨，铜矿 495 万吨，铅矿 597 万吨，锌矿 608 万吨，铝土矿 1.8 亿吨，钨矿 34.5 万吨，金矿 836 吨，银矿 1.5 万吨，硫铁矿 1.8 亿吨，磷矿 10.3 亿吨（表 2-2）。

表2–2　重要矿产勘查新增查明资源储量

矿种	单 位	2013年	2014年
煤　炭	亿吨	673	561
石　油	亿吨	2.0	1.9
天然气	亿立方米	3816.0	4749.6
页岩气	亿立方米	–	266.9
铁　矿	矿石 亿吨	26.5	43
锰　矿	矿石 亿吨	1.1	1.9
铜　矿	金属 万吨	261	495
铅　矿	金属 万吨	446	597
锌　矿	金属 万吨	1389	608
铝土矿	矿石 亿吨	2.4	1.8
金　矿	金属 吨	758	836
银　矿	金属 万吨	1.3	1.5
钨　矿	WO_3 万吨	20.3	34.5
锡　矿	金属 万吨	13	0.87
钼　矿	金属 万吨	461	198
锑　矿	金属 万吨	13.7	24.6

续表

矿种	单位	2013年	2014年
硫铁矿	矿石 万吨	7981	17646
磷　矿	矿石 亿吨	4.4	10.3
钾　盐	KCl 万吨	0	7042

注：石油、天然气、页岩气为探明技术可采储量。

- 表示无统计数据。

二、矿产资源潜力

1. 油气矿产资源潜力

中国的油气资源主要集中在大型含油气盆地。渤海湾、松辽、塔里木、鄂尔多斯、准噶尔、珠江口等主要含油气盆地的石油资源量、储量和产量贡献超过80%。全国常规油气资源潜力评价结果表明：截至2014年底，全国石油地质资源量1085亿吨，可采资源量268亿吨；常规天然气地质资源量68万亿立方米，可采资源量40万亿立方米；页岩气地质资源量134万亿立方米，可采资源量25万亿立方米；煤层气地质资源量36.8万亿立方米，可采资源量10.9万亿立方米。总体上看，中国天然气资源潜力大于石油，将进入天然气储量、产量快速增长的发展阶段。

2. 固体矿产资源潜力

2014年，煤炭、铀、铁、锰、铬、铜、铅、锌、铝、镍、钨、锡、钼、锑、金、银、锂、稀土、菱镁矿、萤石、硫、磷、钾、重晶石、硼等25种矿产的资源潜力评价工作全面完成。资源潜力评价结果表明：我国重要矿产资源查明程度平均为30.3%，找矿潜力巨大。其中，2000米以浅，煤炭预测资源量3.88万亿吨，资源查明率为29.6%；铁矿预测资源量1960亿吨，资源查明率为33.1%；铜矿预测资源量3.04亿吨，资源查明率为29.5%；铝土矿预测资源量179.7亿吨，资源查明率为20.3%（表2-3）。

表2-3　重要矿产资源潜力

序号	矿种	单位	预测资源量	资源查明率/%
1	煤　炭	万亿吨	3.88	29.6
2	铁　矿	矿石 亿吨	1960	33.1

续表

序号	矿种	单位	预测资源量	资源查明率/%
3	锰 矿	矿石 亿吨	35.2	31.7
4	铬铁矿	矿石 万吨	5556	23.6
5	铜 矿	金属 亿吨	3.04	29.5
6	铅 矿	金属 亿吨	2.35	30.5
7	锌 矿	金属 亿吨	5.11	28.9
8	铝土矿	矿石 亿吨	179.7	20.3
9	镍 矿	金属 万吨	2451.4	34.6
10	钨 矿	WO_3 万吨	2973.1	24.6
11	锡 矿	金属 万吨	1861.2	30.7
12	钼 矿	金属 万吨	8960.3	24.9
13	锑 矿	金属 万吨	1518.1	29.1
14	金 矿	金属 万吨	3.27	32.2
15	银 矿	金属 万吨	72.6	36.1
16	硬岩锂	金属 万吨	593.7	36.6
	卤水锂	金属 万吨	9248.1	18.8
17	菱镁矿	矿石 亿吨	131.4	19.1
18	萤 石	矿物 亿吨	9.53	25.7
19	硫铁矿	矿石 亿吨	184	25.9
	自然硫	硫 亿吨	2.3	60.8
20	磷 矿	矿石 亿吨	560	29.3
21	钾 盐	KCl 亿吨	20.0	40.0
22	重晶石	矿石 亿吨	14.4	25.0
23	硼 矿	B_2O_3 亿吨	1.89	33.5

三、矿业权登记

1. 油气矿产矿业权

截至2014年底，全国共有油气矿产探矿权1030个，同比下降3.6%；登记面积393.07万平方千米，同比下降4.9%。油气矿产采矿权705个，同比增长4.4%；登记面积14.31万平方千米，同比增长5.7%。2014年，国土资源部会审批准颁发油气矿产勘查许可证484个，开采许可证36个。

2. 非油气矿产矿业权

2014 年，全国新立非油气矿产探矿权 1269 个，同比下降 4.6%；新增登记勘查面积 3.26 万平方千米，下降 29.2%。新立采矿权 2306 个，增长 17.6%；新增登记开采面积 1165 平方千米，下降 38.7%；新增矿石设计生产规模 5.8 亿吨 / 年，增长 9.7%。2015 年上半年，全国新立非油气矿产探矿权 457 个，同比下降 23.4%；新增登记勘查面积 1.12 万平方千米，下降 9.2%。新立采矿权 1002 个，增长 19.0%；新增登记开采面积 984.89 平方千米，增长 48.4%；新增矿石设计生产规模 2.55 亿吨 / 年，增长 14.4%。

截至 2014 年底，全国共有非油气矿产探矿权 3.0 万个，同比下降 5.2%；登记勘查面积 61.15 万平方千米，下降 9.1%。采矿权 8.2 万个，下降 9.6%；登记开采面积 10.44 万平方千米，下降 1.5%（表 2-4）；矿石设计生产规模 147 亿吨 / 年，与上年持平。

表2-4　截至2014年底中国非油气矿产矿业权情况

项目	数量（个）	同比变化/%	登记面积/万km^2	同比变化/%
探矿权	30480	−5.2	61.15	−9.1
其中：新立	1269	−4.6	3.26	−29.2
采矿权	82450	−9.6	10.44	−1.5
其中：新立	2306	17.6	0.1165	−38.7

第三章 矿产资源勘查

2014 年，中国围绕经济发展新常态下的资源需求，加强基础性工作，充分调动各类地质勘查主体的积极性，继续推进“找矿突破战略行动”。地质勘查投入保持 1145 亿元的较高水平，煤炭、石油、天然气、页岩气、锰、铝土矿、铜、铅、锌、金等重要矿产新增一批资源量。

一、地质勘查投入

2014 年，中国地质勘查投入 1145 亿元，同比下降 5.4%（图 3-1）。其中，财政投入 195 亿元，占全国地质勘查投入的 17.0%；社会投入 950 亿元，占 83.0%。油气矿产地质勘查投入 743 亿元，下降 1.2%，占全国地质勘查投入的 64.9%；非油气矿产地质勘查投入 402 亿元，下降 12.5%，占 35.1%，连续第二年下降（图 3-2）。非油气矿产地质勘查投入中，财政投资 179 亿元，占 44.5%；社会投资 223 亿元，占 55.5%。

2014 年，地质勘查完成钻探工作量 2741 万米，下降 5.4%。

二、能源矿产勘查

1. 煤炭

2014 年新增煤炭大中型矿产地 17 处，勘查新增查明资源储量超过 50 亿吨的煤炭

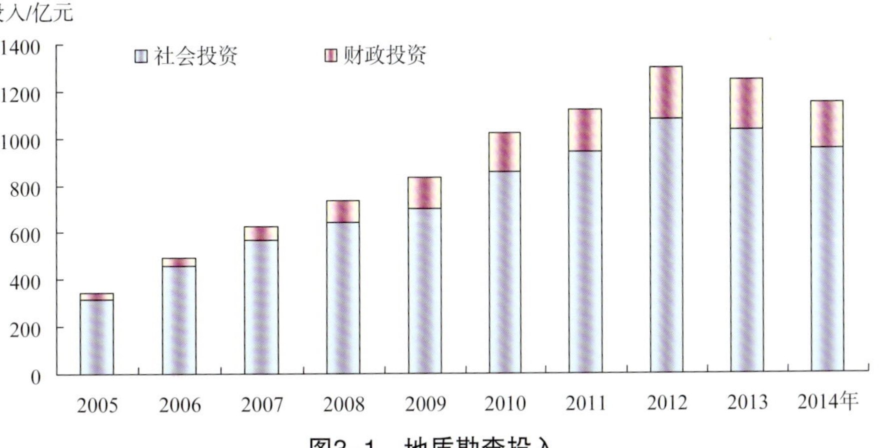

图3-1 地质勘查投入

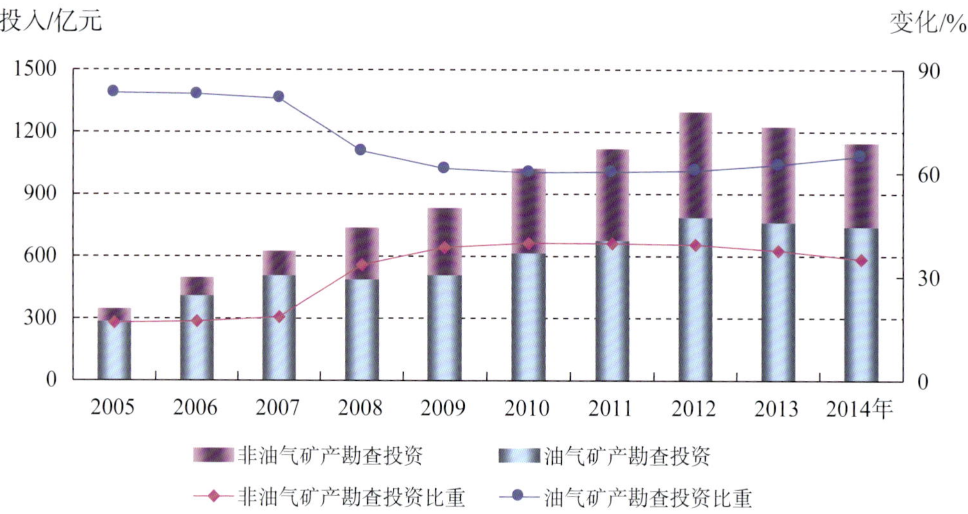

图3-2　油气矿产及非油气矿产地质勘查投入变化

矿产地包括：新疆准东煤田奇台县西黑山矿区红沙泉二号露天煤矿、内蒙古陈旗煤田巴彦哈达勘查区。

2. 常规油气

截至2014年底，石油累计探明地质储量361亿吨，天然气12万亿立方米。2014年，石油新增探明地质储量10.6亿吨，连续第8年超过10亿吨，新增探明地质储量大于1亿吨的油田1个，为中国石油长庆新安边油田。天然气新增探明地质储量9438亿立方米，连续第12年超过5000亿立方米，新增探明地质储量超过千亿立方米的气田5个，分别为中国石油长庆神木气田、中国石油塔里木克拉苏气田、陕西延长延安气田、中国海油湛江陵水17-2气田和中国海油宁波22-1气田。

3. 非常规油气

煤层气：截至2014年底，全国煤层气累计钻井超过1.3万口（其中2014年新增超过1000口，进尺122.2万米）。2014年全国新增探明地质储量602亿立方米，累计探明地质储量6266亿立方米。

页岩气：截至2014年底，页岩气累计勘查投入超过230亿元，钻井780口，形成生产能力13亿立方米。2014年全国新增探明地质储量1068亿立方米，为2011年设定新矿种后首次提交探明地质储量。新探明气田为中国石化勘探涪陵页岩气田。

三、金属与非金属矿产勘查

2014 年，铁矿、铜矿、铅矿、锌矿、铝土矿、钨矿、锡矿、钼矿、锑矿、金矿、银矿、硫铁矿、磷矿和钾盐等 14 种矿产新增查明资源储量主要分布在新疆、云南、山西、内蒙古、河南、山东、贵州、吉林、四川、青海和西藏等省区。其中，勘查新增查明资源储量超过 5 亿吨的铁矿区为辽宁本溪市大台沟铁矿区和山东苍山县兰陵矿区（古林 - 兰陵矿段），超过 1 亿吨的锰矿区为贵州松桃县道坨锰矿，超过 100 万吨的铜矿区为西藏自治区尼木县白容岗讲铜矿，超过 200 万吨的锌矿区为湖南花垣县大脑坡铅锌矿区，超过 3000 万吨的铝土矿区为广西凤山县福家坡矿区铝土矿，超过 100 万吨的镍矿区为青海格尔木市夏日哈木 HS26 号异常区铜镍矿，超过 100 吨的金矿区为新疆乌恰县萨瓦亚尔顿金矿，超过 100 万吨的萤石矿区为浙江省遂昌县柘岱口乡坑西萤石矿矿区，超过 2 亿吨的磷矿为湖北保康县白水河磷矿区。

老矿山深部和外围找矿经济社会效益明显。江苏栖霞山铅锌矿、四川拉拉铜矿、河南老湾金矿等 14 个矿区取得重大找矿突破，估算新增资源储量达到大型矿床规模。39 个矿区取得重要进展。平均延长矿山服务年限 10 年，稳定 12 万职工就业。

专栏 3-1　中央地质勘查基金找矿进展

2014年，中央地质勘查基金项目部署围绕国家能源、资源战略，继续发挥地勘基金在找矿突破战略行动中的衔接拉动作用，充分发挥中央和省级地勘基金的协调联动机制，形成合力，全力助推“找矿突破战略行动”，开展国家级整装勘查区重要矿种的勘查，重点支持煤、铀、铁、铜、钾盐等国家能源和急需紧缺矿产勘查，新发现一批大、中型矿床，煤、铀、铁、钛、钒等矿产资源量有较大幅度提高。2014年新发现大中型矿产地14处，其中大型及以上矿产地5处，中型5处。

四、地下水资源勘查

国土资源部门积极开展乌蒙山区、太行山区、沂蒙山区、柴达木盆地等严重缺水地区水文地质调查工作，通过实施探采结合的方式，施工探采结合水文井 170 多眼，为当地 30 万缺水群众解决了饮水困难。为支援河南、湖北等省抗旱救灾，依托已有水文地质调查项目，应急部署抗旱打井工作，及时公开了 1200 多项水文地质调查成果目

录，供旱区专业地勘队伍抗旱找水打井查询使用，满足抗旱打井技术需求。发布实施《1:5万水文地质调查规范》成为行业标准并发布。2014年全年共完成1:5万水文地质调查图幅100余幅。

第四章　矿产资源开发利用

2014年，中国采矿业固定资产投资保持增长，但增势趋缓，增速为12年以来最低值，占全国固定资产投资的比重下降。其中，煤炭开采和洗选业固定资产投资连续两年负增长。矿产品生产保持增长，但增速明显回落，与基础设施建设相关的原材料如粗钢、十种有色金属、水泥产量增速皆放缓。发布了中国首个矿产资源综合利用评价指标标准，矿产资源综合利用示范基地建设成效显著。

一、采矿业固定资产投资

2014年，中国采矿业固定资产投资额为1.47万亿元，同比增长0.7%，增速回落10.2个百分点，为12年以来最低值。采矿业固定资产投资占全国固定资产投资的2.9%，较上年的3.4%下降0.5个百分点。其中，煤炭开采和洗选业4682亿元，下降9.5%，连续两年负增长；石油与天然气开采业4023亿元，增长6.1%；黑色金属矿采选业1690亿元，增长2.6%；有色金属矿采选业1636亿元，增长2.9%；非金属矿采选业2046亿元，增长13.9%（图4-1）。

2015年上半年，中国采矿业固定资产投资额为5260.50亿元，同比下降7.7%。其

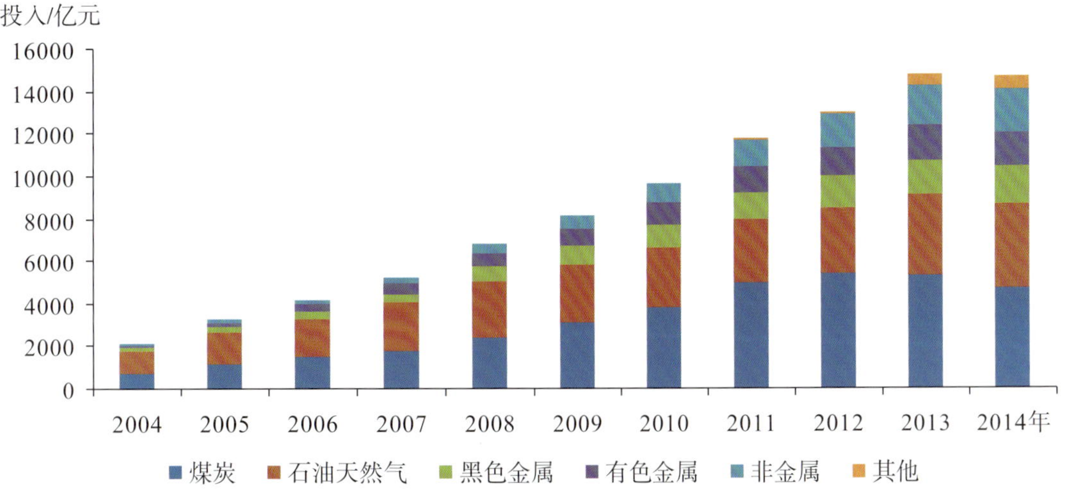

图4-1　采矿业固定资产投资变化

中煤炭开采和洗选业投资1686.05亿元，下降12.8%；石油和天然气开采业1168.95亿元，下降6.5%；黑色金属矿采选业655.81亿元，下降12.8%；有色金属矿采选业628.92亿元，下降5.7%；非金属矿采选业926.22亿元，增长5.4%。

二、矿产品生产与消费

1. 能源生产与消费

中国为世界上第一大能源生产和消费国。2014年，一次能源生产总量为36.0亿吨标准煤，同比增长0.5%（图4-2）；消费总量为42.6亿吨标准煤，增长2.2%；能源自给率为84.5%。能源结构不断改善，煤炭比重不断下降，天然气等清洁能源比重不断上升。2014年能源消费结构为：煤炭占66.0%，水电、风电、核电、天然气等占16.9%。

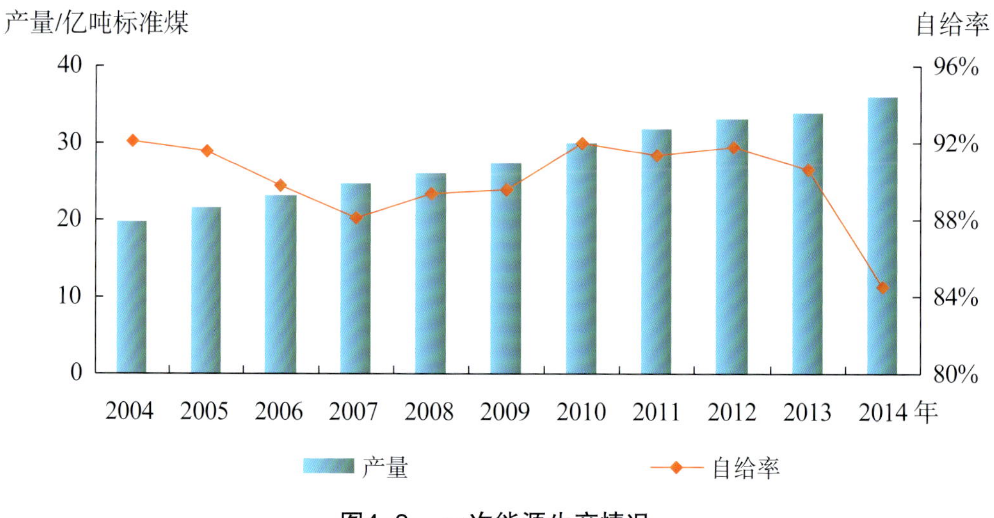

图4-2　一次能源生产情况

2014年，原煤产量38.7亿吨，下降2.5%，连续多年居世界第一位。原油产量2.11亿吨，增长0.7%（图4-3），居第四位。天然气产量1301.6亿立方米，增长7.7%，居第六位。2015年上半年，原油产量1.06亿吨，同比增长2.1%；天然气630亿立方米，增长2.5%。

2. 金属矿产品生产与消费

2014年，生产铁矿石15.1亿吨，同比增长3.9%；粗钢8.2亿吨，增长1.2%（图4-4）；钢材11.3亿吨，增长4.0%。十种有色金属4380.1万吨，增长7.4%；其中精炼

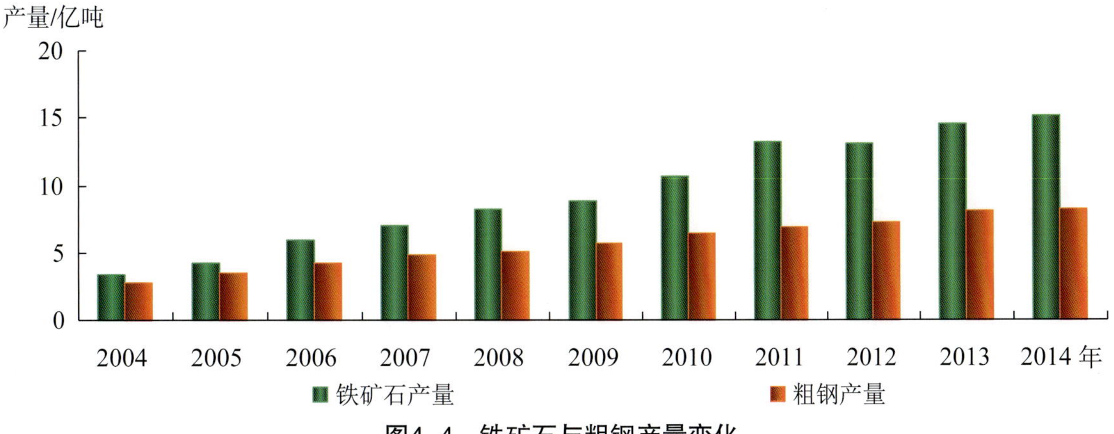

图4-3　原油产量及变化

铜 764.4 万吨，增长 15.0%；电解铝产量 2751.7 万吨，增长 8.2%。黄金产量 458.1 吨，增长 5.5%；消费量 886.09 吨，下降 24.7%。粗钢、十种有色金属、黄金产量均位居全球首位。2015 年上半年，生产铁矿石 6.3 亿吨，同比下降 10.7%；十种有色金属 2526.3 万吨，增长 9.3%；黄金 228.7 吨，增长 8.4%。

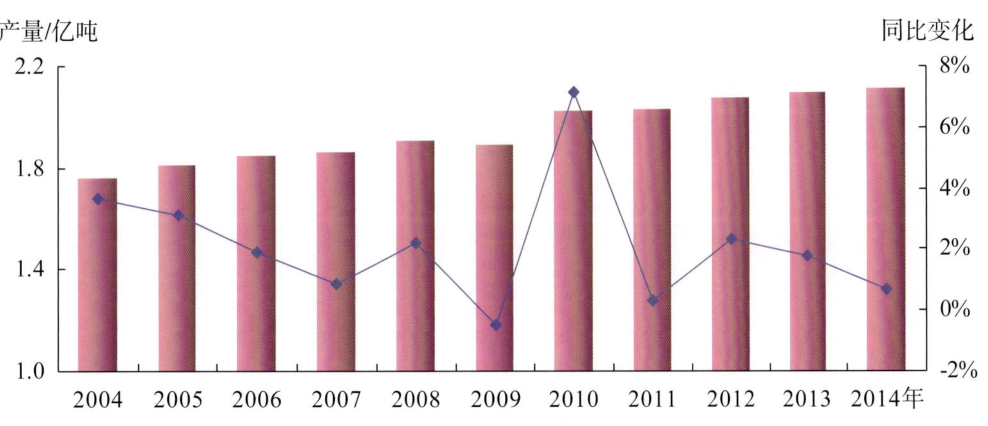

图4-4　铁矿石与粗钢产量变化

3. 非金属矿产品生产

2014 年，生产水泥 24.8 亿吨，同比增长 2.3%（图 4-5）；平板玻璃产量 7.9 亿重量箱，增长 1.1%；钾肥 610.5 万吨（折含 K_2O 100%），增长 13.5%；磷矿石 1.2 亿吨（折含 P_2O_5 30%，下同），增长 7.0%。2015 年上半年，生产水泥 10.8 亿吨，同比减少 5.3%；平板玻璃 4.0 亿重量箱，下降 4.2%；磷矿石 6629.8 万吨，增长 9.1%。

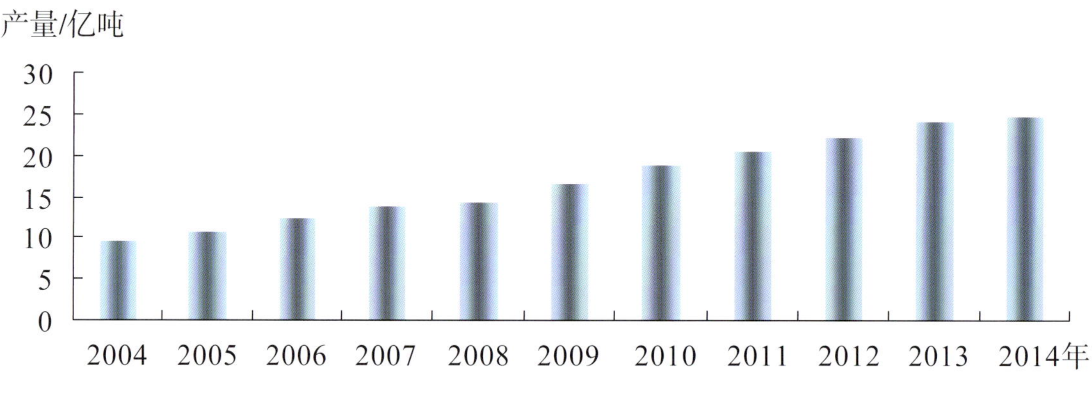

图4–5 水泥产量变化

三、矿产资源节约与综合利用

1. 重要矿产资源综合利用标准体系基本形成

发布首个矿产资源综合利用评价指标标准——《矿产资源综合利用技术指标及其计算方法》（DZ/T 0272—2015），规定了矿产资源综合利用主要技术指标，建立了考核矿产资源利用水平统一要求。发布第三批锰、铬、铝土矿、钨、钼、硫铁矿、石墨和石棉等 8 个矿产资源合理开发利用开采回采率、选矿回收率、综合利用率最低指标要求，连续三年共发布 20 个矿种的开采回采率、选矿回收率、综合利用率指标要求，主要矿种的矿产资源节约与综合利用评价指标体系初步形成。

2. 矿产资源综合利用示范基地建设成效显著

矿产资源综合利用示范基地建设四年多以来，中央财政资金累计投入 148.8 亿元，拉动企业投入资金 949.87 亿元。通过示范基地建设，加速了低渗透超低渗透油气、页岩气、油页岩、钒钛磁铁矿、固体钾盐、低品位胶磷矿等 8 大资源综合利用技术、工艺和装备的革新和产业化应用，使低品位、共伴生和难利用资源变成了经济可采资源，显著提升资源保障能力。

3. 加强技术政策引导约束

印发《矿产资源节约与综合利用鼓励、限制和淘汰技术目录（修订稿）》（国土资发〔2014〕176 号），加强矿产资源节约与综合利用的准入管理，督促企业加大改造力度，逐步淘汰落后产能。

4. 推广先进适用技术

2014 年，国土资源部从矿业行业优选出 60 项先进适用技术予以推广（表 4-1）。三年来，共发布了三批 159 项先进适用技术（油气 22 项、煤炭 34 项、金属矿产 70 项、非金属矿产 33 项）。其中，采矿技术 59 项、选矿技术 40 项、共伴生矿产及尾矿等综合利用技术 60 项。

表4-1　推介的矿产资源综合利用技术

煤炭高效采选和综合利用技术（10项）			
1	煤泥管道输送系统新技术	6	高硫煤矸石高密度重介分选技术
2	水体下厚煤层有效开采技术	7	煤系共伴生油页岩资源综合利用技术
3	极薄煤层高效综采关键技术	8	露天煤矿端帮陡帮开采技术
4	低透气性煤层增透抽采瓦斯技术	9	矿井废弃热源综合利用技术
5	煤泥复合循环流化床洁净焚烧利用技术	10	露天煤矿超薄煤层开采提质技术
油气资源高效开采和综合利用技术（7项）			
11	海相页岩气压裂成套新技术	15	海上平台及陆地终端火炬新型点火系统
12	复杂断块油藏立体开发技术	16	海上薄层油藏自流注水技术
13	浅层超稠油藏双水平井SAGD开发技术	17	空气泡沫驱提高采收率技术
14	水驱废弃油藏CO_2/水交替驱大幅提高采收率技术		
金属高效采选和综合利用技术（29项）			
18	弱磁性矿石高效强磁选关键技术及装备	33	含铜钴尾矿低温焙烧利用技术
19	磁铁矿高压辊终粉磨阶段干选抛尾成套技术及装备	34	高次生铜大型斑岩铜钼矿铜钼分离关键技术
20	镜铁山式难选氧化铁矿提质降杂选矿技术	35	复杂难选低品位镍矿选矿技术
21	无底柱分段崩落法爆破单元实体建模技术	36	露天开采可视化调度管理系统
22	利用低贫锰矿和含硫烟气生产高纯硫酸锰及二氧化锰工艺技术	37	黑白钨矿物强磁分离选别技术
23	破碎难采矿体诱导冒落高效开采技术	38	利用黄金尾矿制备陶瓷釉料和加气混凝土材料
24	大水矿床近顶板灰岩帷幕注浆堵水采矿技术	39	矿山粗骨料高浓度流态管输充填关键技术
25	含磁性矿物工业废渣分选用新型高磁永磁机及综合利用技术	40	铝土矿无传动浮选装备技术
26	复杂隐患空区转换处置及残矿回收技术	41	金尾矿有价金属综合回收技术
27	铁矿尾矿生产新型墙材技术	42	尾矿资源细粒级金属矿物清洁高效回收新技术
28	微细粒难选贫铁矿选矿新工艺	43	尾矿中微细粒钨综合回收技术

续表

金属高效采选和综合利用技术（29项）			
29	悬振锥面选矿机用于金属矿提质降尾技术	44	高碳镍钼矿高效选矿新技术及应用
30	尾矿中铁矿物回收利用技术	45	矽卡岩型铜尾矿活化浮选硫精矿技术
31	尾矿全量资源化综合利用技术	46	液态二氧化硫调控铜与铅锌浮选分离技术
32	铁尾矿磁重分选技术		
非金属高效采选和综合利用技术（14项）			
47	方解石粉体高效加工技术	54	天然脉石英提纯加工技术
48	冷结晶---正浮选生产氯化钾技术	55	磷石膏转化制硫酸铵技术
49	露天废弃矿坑地质环境综合治理与景观建设技术	56	天然碱矿地下溶采与加工技术
50	吸附法从老卤中提锂技术	57	蒙脱石产品深度开发技术
51	低品位石灰石梯级利用技术	58	磷矿高承压含水层下安全高效全尾砂充填采矿技术
52	粉石英生产高纯超细准球形硅微粉和特种二氧化硅新材料技术	59	冶镁白云岩尾矿综合利用新技术
53	低品位含泥固体钾矿脱泥技术	60	机制砂石细粉高效回收与废水循环利用工艺技术

第五章　矿山生态环境建设

矿山地质环境治理恢复投资力度不断加大，矿山开发损毁土地治理恢复成效明显。国家矿山公园数量稳步增长，管理逐步规范化。绿色矿山建设工作全面推进，生态国土建设水平进一步提高。

一、矿山地质环境治理恢复

截至 2014 年底，全国用于矿山地质环境治理资金累计 901.8 亿元，其中中央财政出资 287.3 亿元，安排项目 1954 个，地方财政和企业自筹资金 614.5 亿元。全国矿产开发累计损毁土地 303 万公顷，已完成治理恢复土地 81 万公顷，治理率为 26.7%。其中，利用中央财政资金完成 21.4 万公顷，利用地方财政和企业资金完成 59.6 万公顷。

中央财政资金继续支持资源枯竭型城市矿山地质环境治理工程和矿山地质环境治理示范工程的实施。其中，2014 年下达矿山地质环境治理项目补助资金 17.28 亿元。

截至 2014 年底，全国矿山地质环境治理恢复保证金已缴存 867.7 亿元，占应缴存 1598.7 亿元的 54.3%；全国已缴存矿山 8.59 万个，占应缴存矿山 9.9 万个的 86.8%。采矿权人完成治理义务返还保证金 307.4 亿元。闭坑矿山未履行治理义务，留存保证金 25.2 亿元。

国家矿山公园建设成为矿山地质环境治理恢复的亮点。2005 年以来，共批准了 72 个国家矿山公园建设，已建成开园 30 个。各省（区、市）累计投入矿山公园建设资金 22.9 亿元，建立省级矿山公园 41 个。

2014 年，在安徽潜山、广东佛山、河北泥河湾、宁夏灵武、新疆鄯善等地开展化石发掘。发掘单位按照批准的恢复方案，对涉及的 930 平方米地域进行了严格的环境治理恢复工作。

二、绿色矿业发展

1. 推进绿色矿山试点建设

截至 2014 年底，661 家矿山企业成为国家级绿色矿山试点单位，实现到“十二五”

末国家级试点矿山达600家以上的工作目标，在循环经济发展、资源高效利用、绿色科技引领、矿山生态保护、矿地和谐共赢等方面发挥了示范引导作用。制定了《国家级绿色矿山试点单位验收办法（试行）》，完成山西同煤大唐塔山煤矿等37家首批试点单位的建设进展情况评估，总结了试点成效与问题，研究提出了后续激励政策措施建议。开展了建设标准研究，分行业指导新建和在建绿色矿山建设。

2. 各地积极开展绿色矿山创建工作

各地结合实际情况，有序推进省、市绿色矿山建设。浙江、河北、江西研究制定了绿色矿山管理办法和相关鼓励政策。内蒙古、贵州制定了建设绿色矿山的实施方案。广西、江西和北京编制了绿色矿山建设规划。

第六章　矿产资源管理与政策

依法推进行政审批制度改革，加快政府职能转变，不断提高矿产资源管理科学化、规范化、法治化水平。2014年以来，加大简政放权力度，进一步释放市场活力，共修改了3项行政法规，发布了2项新规章，取消了23项行政审批事项，对矿产资源补偿费和资源税进行了部分调整。

一、矿产资源管理制度变化

1. 修改3项行政法规

2014年7月29日，国务院发布了《国务院关于修改部分行政法规的决定》(国务院令第653号)，与矿产资源管理有关的有：

(1)对《矿产资源勘查区块登记管理办法》的修改：一是删去第十三条第一款中的“经评估确认的”，修改为“申请国家出资勘查并已经探明矿产地的区块的探矿权的，探矿权申请人除依照本办法第十二条的规定缴纳探矿权使用费外，还应当缴纳国家出资勘查形成的探矿权价款”；二是第十三条第二款修改为“国家出资勘查形成的探矿权价款，由具有矿业权评估资质的评估机构进行评估；评估报告报登记管理机关备案”；三是第三十八条修改为“中外合作勘查矿产资源的，中方合作者应当在签订合同后，将合同向原发证机关备案”；四是删去第四十条“从事区域地质调查、区域矿产调查、区域地球物理调查、区域地球化学调查、航空遥感地质调查和区域水文地质调查、区域工程地质调查、区域环境地质调查、海洋地质调查等地质调查工作的，应当向登记管理机关备案。”

(2)对《矿产资源开采登记管理办法》的修改：一是删去《矿产资源开采登记管理办法》第十条第一款中的“经评估确认的”，修改为“申请国家出资勘查并已经探明矿产地的采矿权的，采矿权申请人除依照本办法第九条的规定缴纳采矿权使用费外，还应当缴纳国家出资勘查形成的采矿权价款”；二是第十条第二款修改为“国家出资勘查形成的采矿权价款，由具有矿业权评估资质的评估机构进行评估；评估报告报登记管理机关备案”；三是第二十九条修改为“中外合作开采矿产资源的，中方合作者应当在签订合同后，将合同向原发证机关备案。”

（3）对《探矿权采矿权转让管理办法》的修改：将第九条第二款修改为“国家出资勘查形成的探矿权、采矿权价款，由具有矿业权评估资质的评估机构进行评估；评估报告报探矿权、采矿权登记管理机关备案。”

2. 发布实施2项新规章

（1）发布了《地质环境监测管理办法》

2014 年 4 月 29 日，根据《中华人民共和国矿产资源法》、《地质灾害防治条例》等法律法规，发布了《地质环境监测管理办法》（国土资源部第 59 号令）。规定了地质环境监测的目的、依据、定义、原则、主体、适用范围、法律责任等。

（2）发布了《国土资源行政处罚办法》

2014 年 5 月 7 日，发布了《国土资源行政处罚办法》（中华人民共和国国土资源部令第 60 号）。其核心原则是规范行政权力，保护群众权益。

3. 审批事项变化

（1）取消 23 项审批事项

2014 年以来取消与矿产资源相关的行政审批及非行政审批项目 23 项，包括矿业权投放计划审批、矿业权设置方案审批或备案核准、地质资料延期汇交审批、整装勘查区设置审批、调整矿产勘查风险分类审批、矿业权价款评估备案核准等（表 6-1）。

表6-1　2014年以来取消矿产资源相关审批事项

序号	项目名称	类别	取消调整依据
1	中外合作勘查、开采矿产资源前置性审查	行政许可	《国务院关于取消和下放一批行政审批项目的决定》（国发[2014]5号）
2	地质调查备案核准	行政许可	
3	在国家地质公园的地质遗迹保护区外的园区进行矿产资源勘查、开发和工程建设活动审批[①]	非行政许可审批	
4	矿业权投放计划审批	非行政许可审批	
5	中国温泉之乡（城、都）命名审批	非行政许可审批	
6	煤炭矿业权审批管理改革试点省煤炭矿业权审批项目备案核准	非行政许可审批	

续表

序号	项目名称	类别	取消调整依据
7	跨省、自治区、直辖市销售的矿泉水的注册登记	非行政许可审批	《国务院关于取消和下放一批行政审批项目的决定》（国发[2014]27号）
8	地质资料延期汇交审批	行政许可	《国务院关于取消和调整一批行政审批项目等事项的决定》（国发[2015]11号）
9	矿产地储备区域矿产资源开发利用审批	行政许可	
10	县级以上人民政府有关部门查阅保护期内的地质资料审查	行政许可	
11	省、自治区、直辖市矿山地质环境保护规划审核	行政许可	
12	重点保护古生物化石产地名录审批	行政许可	
13	国土资源部科技平台建设审批	行政许可	
14	整装勘查区设置审批	行政许可	
15	调整矿产勘查风险分类审批	行政许可	
16	水文、水资源调查评价机构资质认定	行政许可	
17	矿产资源综合利用示范基地确定和矿产资源综合利用示范基地建设总体规划审查批准	非行政许可审批	国务院关于取消非行政许可审批事项的决定（国发[2015]27号）
18	探矿权、采矿权协议出让申请审批	非行政许可审批	
19	矿业权设置方案审批或备案核准	非行政许可审批	
20	设立、变更或者撤销国家规划矿区、对国民经济具有重要价值的矿区审批	非行政许可审批	
21	矿业权价款评估备案核准	非行政许可审批	
22	直辖市人民政府申报的中国温泉之乡（城、都）的发展建设总体规划审查	非行政许可审批	
23	国家地质公园规划审批	非行政许可审批	

① 取消国土资源部审批，保留地方政府审批。

（2）保留和调整的审批事项

根据2015年5月6日国务院第91次常务会议审议通过的非行政许可审批事项清理工作意见，将“矿产资源规划审批”、“保护性开采的特定矿种审核”非行政许可审批事项调整为政府内部审批。国土资源部保留9项行政审批事项，包括19个子项（表6-2）。

表6-2 国土资源部目前实施的行政许可审批事项目录

项目编码	项目名称	子项	审批对象
12004	勘查矿产资源审批	1.新设探矿权登记	事业单位、企业
		2.探矿权延续登记	事业单位、企业
		3.探矿权保留登记	事业单位、企业
		4.探矿权注销登记	事业单位、企业
		5.探矿权变更登记	事业单位、企业
		6.勘查石油、天然气等流体矿产试采审批	企业
		7.探矿权转让审批	事业单位、企业
12005	开采矿产资源审批	1.新设采矿权登记	企业
		2.采矿权转让审批	企业
		3.采矿权延续登记	企业
		4.矿区范围划定	企业
		5.采矿权变更登记	企业
		6.采矿权注销登记	企业
		7.矿山地质环境保护与治理恢复方案审批	企业
12006	地质勘查资质审批	无	事业单位、企业
12008	地质资料保护登记	无	事业单位、企业
12009	地质灾害防治单位甲级资质审批	1.地质灾害危险性评估单位甲级资质审批	事业单位、企业
		2.地质灾害治理工程勘查单位甲级资质审批	事业单位、企业
		3.地质灾害治理工程设计单位甲级资质审批	事业单位、企业
		4.地质灾害治理工程施工单位甲级资质审批	事业单位、企业
		5.地质灾害治理工程监理单位甲级资质审批	事业单位、企业
12010	重点保护古生物化石发掘审批	无	事业单位、企业、社会组织
12011	收藏单位之间转让、交换、赠与其收藏的重点保护古生物化石审批	无	事业单位、企业、社会组织

续表

项目编码	项目名称	子项	审批对象
12012	重点保护古生物化石进出境审批	无	事业单位、企业、社会组织
12044	国土资源部质量监督检测中心认定	无	事业单位

二、矿产资源税费

1. 税费政策调整

根据财政部《关于实施煤炭资源税改革的通知》(财税 [2014]72 号)、《关于调整原油、天然气资源税有关政策的通知》(财税 [2014]73 号) 和《关于全面清理涉及煤炭原油天然气收费基金有关问题的通知》(财税 [2014]74 号) (2014 年 10 月) 要求，自 2014 年 12 月 1 日起，将全国煤炭、原油、天然气矿产资源补偿费费率降为零，在全国范围内实施煤炭资源税从价计征改革，清理相关收费基金，计征方法实行从价定率计征。原油、天然气资源税适用税率由 5% 提高至 6%。2015 年 4 月，财政部、国家发展改革委联合发布《关于清理涉及稀土、钨、钼收费基金有关问题的通知》(财税 [2015]53 号)，决定自 2015 年 5 月 1 日起，在全国范围统一将稀土、钨、钼矿产资源补偿费费率降为零，停止征收稀土、钨、钼价格调节基金 (表 6-3、6-4)。

表6-3　矿产资源补偿费费率（2015年）

矿　种	费率（%）
石油、天然气、煤炭、稀土、钨、钼	0
湖盐、岩盐、天然卤水	0.5
煤层气、石煤、油砂	1
天然沥青、油页岩；铁、锰、铬、钒、钛；铜、铅、锌、铝土矿、镍、钴、锡、铋、汞、锑、镁；溴、砷	2
铀、钍、地热；铌、钽、铍、锂、锆、锶、铷、铯；锗、镓、铟、铊、铪、铼、镉、硒、碲；二氧化碳气、硫化氢气、氦气、氡气	3
金、银、铂、钯、钌、锇、铱、铑；离子型稀土；宝石、玉石、宝石级金刚石；矿泉水	4
其他矿产	2

表6-4　资源税税目税率表(2014年起)

税目		调整后税率
一、原油		销售额的6%
二、天然气		销售额的6%
三、煤炭	焦煤	销售额的2%～10%（由地方政府制定）
	其他煤炭	
四、其他非金属矿原矿	普通非金属矿原矿	每吨或者每立方米0.5～20元
	贵重非金属矿原矿	每千克或者每克拉0.5～20元
五、黑色金属矿原矿		每吨2～30元
六、有色金属矿原矿	稀土矿	每吨0.4～60元
	其他有色金属矿原矿	每吨0.4～30元
七、盐	固体盐	每吨10～60元
	液体盐	每吨2～10元

2. 税费征收

2014 年，全国矿产资源补偿费征收入库金额为 197.37 亿元，同比下降 8.4%；资源税收入 1083.6 亿元，增长 7.8%。

三、矿产资源规划

1. 全面启动第三轮矿产资源规划编制工作

由国土资源部会同国家发改委、财政部、工业和信息化部、环境保护部、商务部等有关部门共同开展第三轮矿产资源规划编制，并对省市县各级规划编制工作做出全面部署。

2. 完成第三轮矿产资源规划顶层设计

根据全面深化改革和国土资源管理工作新要求，加强顶层设计，提出第三轮矿产资源规划总体思路，明确各级规划功能定位和主要任务，强化矿产资源规划分区管理制度、矿种差别化管理政策，对矿产资源勘查开发、矿山地质环境治理等规划目标、重点项目、重大工程进行了论证。

3. 指导推动地方各级规划编制

制定《省级矿产资源总体规划编制技术规程》和《市县级矿产资源总体规划编制指导意见》，明确地方各级规划编制要求。目前，31 个省（区、市）已相继开展了规划专题研究、重要指标和重大工程的论证工作，并在此基础上提出了各省级规划大纲。

四、矿业权管理

1. 加大简政放权力度

继 2013 年取消整装勘查区矿业权设置方案审查、申请国家出资从事区域性矿产地质调查的地区暂停受理新的探矿权备案核准等 2 项审批事项的基础上，又新取消了 10 项与矿业权管理相关审批事项（表 6-1）。

2. 强化市场调节

一是取消“暂停受理新设煤探矿权申请”，煤炭新立探矿权有序投放。自 2014 年 9 月 12 日实施该政策至 2015 年 6 月 30 日，新立探矿权 35 个；二是停止下达锑矿开采总量控制指标；三是将钨矿综合利用指标由约束性改为指导性；四是调整“暂停受理新设稀土矿业权管理政策”，对国家确定符合“开采总量控制、采储平衡”要求的大型稀土企业集团，允许新设稀土探矿权、采矿权。

3. 强化矿业权审批公示公开

严格执行矿业权出让转让公开制度，实行矿业权出让转让基本信息公示公开。2014 年以来在国土资源部门户网站公示公开基本信息 1.46 万项，累计 6.02 万项；公告矿业权登记结果信息 5.4 万项，累计 24.1 万项。

通过国土资源部门户网站向社会提供矿业权登记信息查验服务，2014 年以来共查验 13.4 万次，累计 38.6 万次。

五、地质勘查资质管理

1. 地质勘查资质概况

截至 2014 年底，全国 2574 个地勘单位共持有各类各级地质勘查资质 7336 个，其中：甲级资质 2658 个，乙级资质 2800 个，丙级资质 1878 个。1106 个单位有甲级资质，

744 个单位有乙级资质，724 个单位有丙级资质；有甲级资质的国有地勘单位 885 个。

全国地勘单位资质类别构成：区域地质调查 396 个，海洋地质调查 16 个，石油天然气矿产勘查 4 个，液体矿产勘查 660 个，气体矿产勘查 276 个，固体矿产勘查 1925 个，水文地质、工程地质、环境地质调查 1028 个，地球物理勘查 773 个，地球化学勘查 364 个，航空地质调查 5 个，遥感地质调查 84 个，地质钻（坑）探 1344 个，地质实验测试 461 个（图 6-1）。

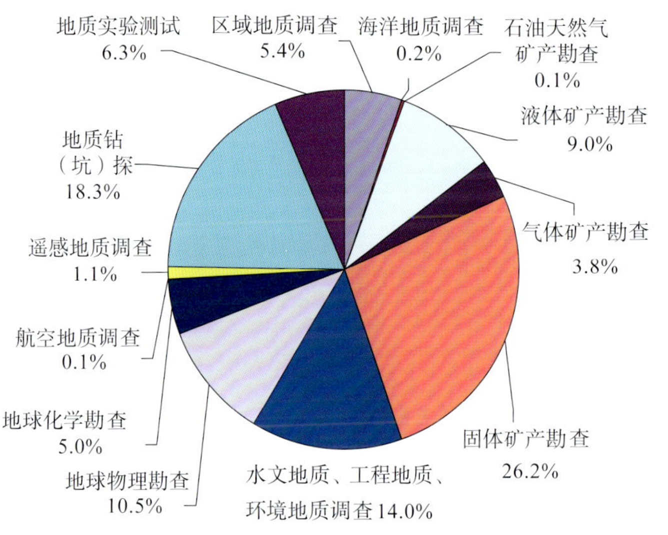

图6-1　全国地质勘查单位资质类别构成

地勘单位按经济类型划分为：国有 1268 个，集体 21 个，股份合作 12 个，有限责任 1129 个，股份有限 63 个，私营 55 个，其它 21 个，合资经营（港或澳、台资）1 个，港、澳、台商独资经营 1 个，外资 2 个，外商投资股份有限公司 1 个（图 6-2）。

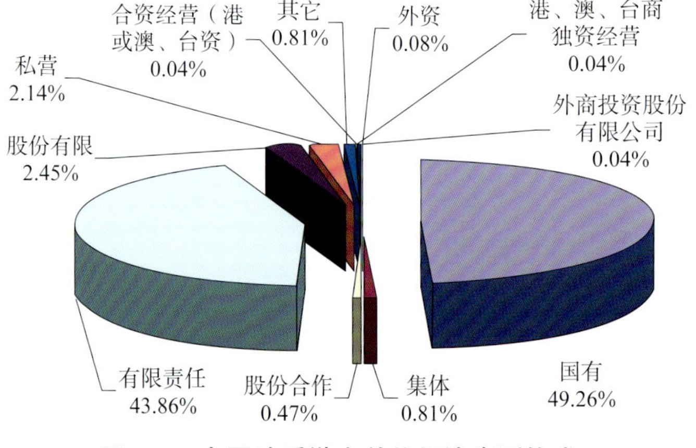

图6-2　全国地质勘查单位经济类型构成

2. 地质勘查资质审批

国土资源部完成了 2014 年地质勘查资质新设、延续申请集中受理、报批及公告，勘查资质变更、补证、注销申请日常受理审批及公告，共颁发地质勘查资质证书 389 个（其中：新设 196 个，延续 29 个，变更 164 个）、注销地质勘查资质证书 3 个。

第七章　地质矿产调查评价与地质资料服务

2014 年，地质矿产调查评价与地质资料服务在经济社会发展中的先行性和基础性作用更加凸显，为经济社会发展和生态文明建设提供了重要支撑和保障。地质调查成果丰硕，为国家矿产资源安全提供了重要保障。加快地质大数据信息资源汇聚和地质信息共享服务平台建设，地质资料信息服务能力和水平进一步提升。

一、基础地质调查

1. 区域地质调查

2014 年，完成 1 ： 5 万区域地质调查 21.6 万平方千米，累计完成 304.6 万平方千米，占陆域国土面积的 31.7%。完成 1 ： 25 万区域地质修测 2.2 万平方千米，累计完成 593.5 万平方千米，占陆域国土面积的 61.7%。

2. 区域地球物理调查

2014 年，完成 1 ： 5 万航空磁测 23 万平方千米，重点成矿区带工作程度提高到 49%。完成 1 ： 5 万磁法测量、区域重力测量、电法测量分别为 5.1 万、2.4 万和 0.4 万平方千米。完成 1 ： 25 万区域重力测量 19 万平方千米，陆域工作程度提高到 59%。

3. 区域地球化学调查

2014 年，完成 1 ： 5 万区域化探 24 万平方千米，重点成矿区带工作程度提高到 35%。完成 1 ： 25 万区域化探 5.1 万平方千米，陆域工作程度提高到 66%。

4. 遥感地质调查

在祁连山成矿带西段获取 2000 余平方千米航空高光谱数据，制作了正射校正产品，并提取了矿物信息。在东昆仑、阿尔金、班公湖－怒江成矿带部分地区开展 5020 平方千米矿产资源高精度遥感调查。

5. 海洋地质调查

继续开展我国管辖海域 1 ： 100 万海洋区域地质调查、重点海域 1 ： 25 万海洋区

域地质调查和 1 ： 5 万海洋区域地质调查试点、重点海岸带综合地质调查与监测、海域油气资源调查、天然气水合物资源勘查以及大洋科学考察等工作。其中，1 ： 100 万海洋区域地质调查 16 个图幅的外业调查工作全部完成，首次实现我国管辖海域区域地质调查全覆盖。

二、矿产资源调查评价

1. 常规油气资源调查评价

以新区、新层系、新类型、新认识为重点，兼顾主要含油气盆地综合研究、整体评价和盆地多种能源综合调查评价，取得了一系列重要成果。

新区调查开辟了新阵地。西藏伦坡拉盆地实施地震勘探发现 3 个岩性圈闭，为羌塘盆地油气勘探提供战略储备；南祁连盆地东北部木里地区发现褐色原油，展现出多种能源综合勘查广阔前景。

新层系调查锁定一批新目标。松辽外围突泉盆地“突参 1 井”钻获轻质原油，在东北地区中下侏罗统获得重要新发现，准噶尔南缘博格达地区二叠系发现含油气岩层，开辟油气勘探新领域。

基础地质调查取得重要新认识。羌塘盆地优选出 9 个重点区块，西部大型盆地碳酸盐岩油气调查圈定了 6 个重点有利区块，经后续勘探验证，四川盆地中西部三叠系、鄂尔多斯盆地奥陶系、塔中下寒武系取得重大进展，优选油气招标区块，有力支撑新疆油气体制改革。

2. 非常规油气资源调查评价

煤层气调查优选出 28 个盆地群、56 个有利区带。松辽外围发现优质油页岩，鄂尔多斯南部渭北隆起钻获厚层油砂。

南方海相页岩气调查取得实质性进展，湘西北牛蹄塘组、黔南打屋坝组解析出含量较高的页岩气。北方页岩气调查拓宽陆相和海陆过渡相新领域：鄂尔多斯盆地南部延长组发现高含气量页岩层段；河南“尉参 1 井”发现多层气测异常。通过综合调查评价，优选出 42 个有利区块，为页岩气区块招标提供了依据。

3. 铀矿资源调查评价

截至 2014 年底，已系统评价北方伊犁、鄂尔多斯等 13 个盆地的砂岩铀矿成矿远

景及南方桃山 - 诸广、赣杭带、雪峰山 - 摩天岭等重要铀成矿区带主要铀矿田外围的资源潜力，完成铀矿地质调查 60 多万平方千米。筛查煤田勘查区 500 余个，排查煤田和石油钻孔 3 万余个，筛选出潜在铀矿孔约 1500 个，潜在矿化孔 1400 个，找矿靶区 200 余个，新发现二十余处矿产地及矿点。

4. 地热资源调查评价

全面完成 256 个地级市浅层地温能调查评价和 31 个省（区、市）地热资源调查与区划。西藏措美县古堆 230 米深度钻获 215℃高温地热，显示了良好的资源前景。青海贵德 3050 米深度钻获 150℃干热岩，实现我国干热岩勘查零的突破。

5. 非能源矿产资源调查评价

完成 1 ∶ 5 万矿产地质调查 5 万平方千米。圈定物化探异常 6300 处，发现矿（化）点 1000 余处，圈定找矿靶区 300 余处，新发现矿产地 35 处。西藏改则舍拉玛地区新发现超大型铜金铁多金属矿化带。新疆东天山麓北发现大型远景规模铜镍矿。青海东昆仑牙扎曲发现大型规模金矿化带。湖南大万金矿外围钻探证实具有超大型金矿找矿前景。广东始兴发现 20 万吨资源远景钨锡矿。西藏罗布莎南部提交 200 万吨铬铁矿资源量，西藏香卡山矿区新发现铬铁矿体，估算新增资源量 25 万吨，有望实现千万吨级资源基地。青海柴达木盆地新增 1 亿吨氯化钾远景资源。四川甲基卡外围新增 64 万吨氧化锂资源量，达到超大型规模。湖南城步发现 18 条高纯石英矿脉，含量大于 99%。湖北宜昌新发现 2 处晶质石墨中型矿产地，湖北竹溪发现近百万吨远景铌矿化带。

三、地质资料管理与服务

1. 地质资料汇交监管明显加强

（1）成果地质资料汇交量持续增加

2014 年，全国共汇交地质资料 14827 份。其中，矿产地质和水工环类资料分别占汇交总量的 42.8% 和 47.4%；油气地质资料汇交 604 份，较上年增长 17.7%。截至 2014 年底，部、省两级地质资料馆藏机构地质资料总量共 45.95 万份，增长 3.7%。

（2）原始地质资料汇交量稳步增长

2014 年，各省（区、市）地质资料馆藏机构共接收原始地质资料 2062 份，较上年

增加 78%。油气等委托保管单位共接收 19.19 万份原始地质资料。截至 2014 年底，委托保管的原始地质资料达到近 60 万份，增长 17%。

(3) 实物地质资料馆藏品种不断丰富

采集矿产地质、区域地质调查等实物地质资料 35 类，国土资源实物地质资料中心共保管 557 个钻孔的 29.82 万米岩心、40814 件薄片等实物地质资料。2014 年，受委托保管油气等地质资料单位共接收 8.99 万米岩心、25.07 万袋岩屑等实物地质资料，委托保管的实物地质资料为 19.4 万米岩心、300.48 万袋岩屑。

(4) 资料汇交全面实现网上监管

截至 2014 年底，全国地质资料汇交监管平台已入库 20 多万条矿业权及地质工作项目数据，以及 7 万多种已汇交的成果、原始、实物资料相关信息。

2. 地质资料社会化服务成效显著

(1) 共享服务平台取得显著进展

2014 年各省（区、市）国土资源主管部门的地质资料馆藏机构及国土资源部信息中心、全国地质资料馆、国土资源实物地质资料中心共 34 个节点已全面建成，“分散式保管、网络化服务”的体系基本形成，并向全社会提供非涉密地质资料信息服务。

截至 2014 年底，地质资料共享服务平台全年累计访问量近 62 万次，共有 35.8 万档资料在线提供目录服务，比上年新增了 1.9 万档。

(2) 社会化服务水平进一步提升

2014 年，全国地质资料馆和 31 个省(区、市)地质资料馆藏机构共接待到馆服务 2.55 万人次，提供资料服务 10.1 万份次，国土资源实物地质资料中心共接待服务 5646 人次。受委托保管油气等地质资料单位共接待到馆服务 8321 人次，提供原始地质资料服务 2.66 万份次。

(3) 服务产品不断丰富

2014 年，向社会提供 2565 幅 1∶5 万矿产资源调查成果服务工作。通过全国重要地质钻孔服务平台公开发布了全国 90 万个地质钻孔的基础信息及 5 万个钻孔柱状图信息，公开发布了 1∶50 万水工环调查成果系列图数据、全国 109 片整装勘查区地学文献专题数据、《京津冀国土资源与环境地质图集》、《中国自然资源图集》等。

(4) 数字化服务产品显著增加

部、省两级地质资料馆藏机构继续大力推进地质资料数字化工作，馆藏资料中电

子文档数量达到40.49万份，占馆藏资料总量的88.1%。天津、河北等15个省（区、市）已将馆藏资料全部数字化。馆藏地质资料数字化工作有力支撑了共享服务平台和电子阅览室建设，促进了电子数据的借阅利用。2014年部、省两级地质资料馆藏机构电子数据复制量为3.87万份次。

第八章 科技创新与国际合作

2014 年以来，矿产资源科技创新与国际合作取得积极进展。新一代中国地层表正式发布实施，研发出一批地质勘查新装备。发布了 12 项国家标准和 75 项推荐性地质矿产行业标准，进一步提升地质矿产技术标准对矿产资源勘查、开发、管理的支撑能力。成功召开亚太经合组织第五届矿业部长会议等国际矿业会议，深化地质与矿产资源领域的双边、多边国际合作与交流。

一、基础地质与矿产理论研究

1. 新一代中国地层表正式发布实施

《中国地层表（2014）》及《中国地层指南及中国地层指南说明书》(2014 年版) 的修订是在 2001 年版的基础上，充分反映了十几年来中国地层学研究成果，同时参考了国际地层学研究的最新进展。经国土资源部批准（国土资〔2014〕374 号），已公开出版发行。

2. 华夏地块龙泉地区发现亚洲最古老锆石

在华夏地块龙泉岩群云母石英片岩首次发现两颗冥古宙碎屑锆石，其中一颗为亚洲最古老的锆石，年龄为 41.27 亿年。

3. 揭示华北古老大陆地壳结构及演化过程

在冀东地区发现大量 38 亿～ 35 亿年形成的碎屑锆石，在鞍山地区发现 38 亿～ 31 亿年多期岩浆活动，证明鄂尔多斯地块强烈卷入古元古代晚期构造热事件，首次在华北克拉通划分出三个年龄大于 26 亿年的古陆块，深化了华北克拉通早期地壳演化、壳幔相互作用及沉积变质铁矿的认识。

4. 汶川地震断裂作用研究取得重要成果

首次记录到大地震后断裂快速愈合过程信息，完善了地震断裂理论，对深化认识汶川地震机理具有重要意义。

二、矿产资源勘查开发技术

1. 研发出一批地质勘查新装备

研制了一套国产化率为90%的深海无人遥控作业系统（简称海马号），并在我国南海某海域通过了4502米海试。研制出ZSM-6型电子重力仪原理样机，全面实现智能化。同位素地质学专用TOF-SIMS科学仪研制成功，设计出一套多次反射质量分析器，实现了一次离子初步在样品表面聚焦及离子束脉冲化轰击样品，并检测到二次离子信号。研制成功达到国际先进水平的Φ2000全回转套管钻机，创下国内卵砾石层全回转套管钻进深度纪录。

2. 地质勘查方法技术体系进一步完善

开发出功能齐全的拥有自主知识产权的航空物探数据处理系统（GeoProbe Mager）。完善了海洋地球化学调查配套技术方法，建立了近海沉积物地球化学组分分析配套分析方案，建立了一系列配套技术方法。攻克了无人机可靠性、大数据实时传输、山区通讯链路中继、数据快速处理等关键技术，初步建立了无人机遥感应急监测技术体系。

3. 应用示范有效促进技术装备实用化

无人机航空物探系统进一步完善，达到实用化水平。大深度三维电磁勘探系统立体探测示范取得成功。

4. 矿产资源综合利用技术得到深度应用

稀土矿“浮团聚磁选”新工艺研发及产业化获得重大进展。滇渝地区低品位铝土矿选矿技术取得重大进展，研究和开发了新型的浮硫起泡剂和活化剂，大大提高了浮硫的选择性，实现了铝土矿中硫的高效利用。

三、地质矿产技术标准

2014年以来，发布实施了《铜矿石、铅矿石和锌矿石化学分析方法》等12项国家标准（表8-1）和《页岩气资源/储量计算与评价技术规范》等75项推荐性地质矿产行业标准，进一步提升地质矿产技术标准对矿产资源勘查、开发、管理的支撑能力。

表8-1　2014年以来发布的地质矿产相关国家标准

国家标准代码	国家标准名称
GB/T 16950-2014	地质岩心钻探钻具
GB/T 30712-2014	抛光钻石质量测量允差的规定
GB/T 30713-2014	砚石 显微鉴定方法
GB/T 30714-2014	电感耦合等离子体质谱法测定砚石中的稀土元素
GB/T 14353.13-2014	铜矿石、铅矿石和锌矿石化学分析方法 第13部分：镓量、铟量、铊量和钼量测定
GB/T 14353.14-2014	铜矿石、铅矿石和锌矿石化学分析方法 第14部分：锗测定
GB/T 14353.15-2014	铜矿石、铅矿石和锌矿石化学分析方法 第15部分：硒测定
GB/T 14353.17-2014	铜矿石、铅矿石和锌矿石化学分析方法 第17部分：铊测定
GB/T 14353.18-2014	铜矿石、铅矿石和锌矿石化学分析方法 第18部分：铜量、铅量、锌量、钴量、镍量测定
GB/T 958-2015	区域地质图图例
GB/T3 1390 -2015	观赏石鉴评
GB/T3 1432-2015	独山玉 命名与分类

四、国际合作

1. 拓展矿业领域国际合作

一是成功召开亚太经合组织第五届矿业部长会议、2014 中国国际矿业大会和 2014 中国 - 东盟矿业合作论坛，举办了中国（长沙）国际矿物宝石博览会。二是与美国、阿根廷、智利、墨西哥地质矿产合作纳入双边合作总体框架。加强与美国在页岩气勘查开发领域的合作，共同召开中美非常规油气资源可持续发展论坛。召开了中墨矿业合作工作组第四次会议。三是巩固了与加拿大、澳大利亚、俄罗斯、南非等传统矿业大国的合作，在完善部际对话合作机制、推动矿业投资经贸合作、加强科技与信息交流等方面形成了系列合作成果。四是拓展了与中亚、东南亚、拉美、非洲等地区新型经济体的合作，与乌兹别克斯坦、哈萨克斯坦、印度尼西亚、波兰等国在页岩气开发利用、地球化学调查、地质资料共享等方面达成了合作意向。

2. 加强科技领域国际合作

一是积极推动联合国教科文组织在中国地质科学院地球物理地球化学勘探研究所设立全球尺度地球化学国际研究中心，推动“为后代提供资源”倡议计划。二是主办第三届世界滑坡论坛、第八届国际盐湖学会等重要国际学术会议，提升中国地学的国际影响力。三是成立了中国 - 上海合作组织地学合作研究中心，为上合组织成员国加强地学领域合作搭建了重要平台。